THE LoveTeam GAME PLAN

How a Loving Couple can Think, Speak, and Act Like a Team

Copyrighted Material

The LoveTeam Game Plan
Copyright © 2013 by Richard and Denice Brown

ALL RIGHTS RESERVED
No part of this publication may be reproduced, stored in a retrieval system or transmitted, in any form or by any means—electronic, mechanical, photocopying, recording or otherwise—without prior written permission, except for the inclusion of brief quotations in a review.

For information about this title or to order other books and/or electronic media, contact the publisher:
Richard and Denice Brown
Surprise, Arizona
LoveTeamGamePlan.com
loveteamgameplan@gmail.com

ISBN: 978-0-9885579-0-1
eBook ISBN: 978-0-9885579-1-8

Printed in the United States of America

Cover and Interior design by: 1106 Design
Editors: Rabia Tredeau
   Leslie Fountain
Back Cover Photo: Dreamcatcher's Photography

Table of Contents

Introduction	v
Part One: The Game Plan	1
1. Snapshots of a LoveTeam	9
2. "The Snapshots"	11
3. A Wonderful Example	15
Part Two: The Power of Team	21
Team Spirit	29
4. "We" not "Me"	31
5. Do and Be Our Best	37
6. An Optimistic Attitude	43
7. Support Without Regrets	51
Team Fundamentals	57
8. Basic Principles	59
9. Commitment and a Climate of Trust	65
10. Healthy Habits are Vital	71
11. Momentum and Trends	77
Team Completion	83
12. Unify Our Needs	85
13. Enjoy Our Differences	93
14. Making Changes and Adjustments	99
15. Balance	107

Part Three: The Power of Love 115
   Our Lives Together 121
      16. Best Friends 123
      17. Remember When 131
      18. Fun and Excitement 137
      19. Building a Life Together 145
   I Love You 151
      20. Kindness 153
      21. Affection 159
      22. Appreciation 165
      23. Respect 171
   Relating to Each Other 177
      24. What Makes Us Tick? 179
      25. Communication 185
      26. Cooperative Solutions 191
      27. Forgive and Forget 201
   End Notes 207

Introduction

We believe that committed couples are in need of a new approach for their relationship. Any couple can benefit from the far-reaching concepts that will be presented. Forming a long-lasting closeness will be the exciting result. The statistics sadly suggest that the current and past approaches to having a successful marriage haven't worked, and these percentages most likely apply to other couple relationships as well.

For example, according to the 2010 census, 51 percent of the adult population in the United States is married. In addition, an average of nearly six thousand couples get married every day. For each couple, their wedding is near perfect, their honeymoon is a dream come true, and their hopes for the future are high. They have no doubt, as they take their vows, that their union will be a success and they will grow old happily together. Yes, they know there will be some bumps in the road, but since their love is so strong, they have no hesitation they will weather every obstacle with ease.

However, according to several studies, 95 percent of couples have expressed a decline in happiness and satisfaction in their first ten years of marriage.[1] Sadly, close to 50 percent of couples get divorced. Many of these people found that the glamour of the "honeymoon" period didn't last. Some of them found that they couldn't solve most of their conflicts and that adversity pulled them apart. Or that their relationship had became boring and they took each other for granted. The reality is that their life together was obviously not what they had expected.

Most couples only practice trial-and-error methods to solve their problems. Even when they try counseling or read other self-help relationship books, they lack direction. Others ask their friends, family or spiritual leaders for guidance to improve their union. In many cases, what they receive is a random list of non-related ideas that don't lead them to a practical plan of action.

So how can unhappy couples return to being happy? The exciting answer is that when love is combined with team, they become a LoveTeam! This can bring the continuous joy that couples dream of when they promise to "love, honor and cherish, until death do us part." Most books about relationships start by defining the many problems couples might encounter, then follow by explaining how to solve them. This is crisis management. These books teach being reactive to problems after they occur, rather than ways to prevent difficulties from happening in the first place.

We've found that it's better to have a fence at the top of a cliff, rather than an ambulance at the bottom. So our book will show proactive ways of avoiding problems before they occur, as well as how to manage existing ones. We will inspire you to applaud each of your individual differences, and to become even closer to each other when going through adversity. All of these concepts, plus more, are what we call having a *LoveTeam Game Plan*.

In Part One we'll present "Snapshots" of how a great partnership looks. We all need a model to give us direction, since unfortunately we see so few examples of successful unions in our society. Let these examples be motivators to spur you on, to understand what you may be missing in life. We'll also address the legacy we leave for our children and others around us when we model a close relationship.

Part Two is the "Power of Team." In these twelve chapters, you'll find the ways that great teams are developed: team spirit or attitude, team fundamentals or skills, and how the members of a team complete each other. We will clarify how these relate to your relationship, not about how to form a sports or a business team (even though this information could help these organizations as well).

"The Power of Love" is Part Three. Since players on a sports team wouldn't be encouraged to hold hands, say "I love you," or kiss team members, you'll see that there are certainly wonderful, loving aspects of a LoveTeam that go above and beyond any other team. The chapters in this Part will open your eyes to how you can take love to a new level.

Some of you may feel that your twosome is "comfortable" the way it is. However, being comfortable may mean that you live mostly separate lives. Or that your differences of opinion are no longer discussed because they have usually turned into conflict. Would you like to resolve your problems and bring back the closeness and romance you had previously?

In athletics, it's expected that new players make any necessary changes asked of them to adapt to their new team. So an important question to be asked of you reading this book is, "Are you coachable?" In other words, are you both open to a new action plan? If both of you answered yes, then studying this book will answer the question: "How do we have a great relationship?"

We strongly suggest that you, as a couple, read this book together. However, it can initially be read by only one of you, with the hope that eventually the other will gain the desire to study it as well when they see the positive changes.

When you both acquire the longing and commitment to have the type of relationship you used to dream of, and have the willingness to put these concepts into action, then you'll enjoy a lasting, joyful union with your lifelong mate. They will, once again, seem like the person with whom you fell in love, and the feeling will be mutual. At that point, you will have become a LoveTeam!

Part One

The Game Plan

XOXO

*Goals are dreams we convert to plans
and take action to fulfill.*

~Zig Ziglar

To accomplish anything exceptional and worthwhile, it's conventional wisdom that a goal first needs to be determined. In the words of Aristotle: "Man is a goal-seeking animal. His life only has meaning if he is reaching out and striving for his goals." Because most couples haven't set goals for their relationship, it's no wonder many have a difficult time attaining this meaning in their partnership.

Think of the most successful people in our society who have achieved something worthwhile. For instance, a winning NASCAR driver needs to have a racing team behind him or her to achieve the primary goal to take first place. A Fortune 500 company might have as their main goal to gain the most profits for their shareholders.

We would suggest that the most important goal every committed couple has or should have is to have a great relationship, what we call a "LoveTeam." This goal is very simple and understandable. It's important to ask yourselves now, "Are we willing to do what it takes to have a successful relationship?" If you need to put this book down and discuss this very important question together, please do so.

If you're still reading, then we know you desire to do what's necessary to be successful in your relationship. We're going to guide you in taking the next steps.

The Plan

To meet the goal of becoming a LoveTeam, we have developed a plan to achieve that goal and call it *The LoveTeam Game Plan*. The term "game plan" is commonly used on certain types of teams, including sports teams. There are also business plans in the corporate area and care plans in the medical world, as well as other types of plans to achieve goals.

What is this plan? *The LoveTeam Game Plan* is *for a loving couple to think, speak, and act like a team.* Sounds simple, but it may not be easy for those who haven't had much experience being on a team. Why could it be harder for these people? Because they don't have the first-hand knowledge of how a team works. Additionally, teamwork has never been made clear as a way for success in personal relationships. But team building is a basic component of our society, as in corporations, volunteer organizations, and emergency crews, to name just a few. And it's becoming more essential every day.

After a team decides the main goal, a workable action plan needs to be designed to attain the goal. For example, a farmer doesn't decide that he wants to harvest 100,000 bushels in a season without first having a general plan of how to meet that goal.

As important as it is for couples to have a stated goal to have a great partnership and a plan, it's also vital for them to form a team. Therefore, we have introduced a new word and suggested another way to state the goal, and this is to become a "LoveTeam."

This new term combines the multifaceted concepts of love with the proven concepts of teamwork. This is important because when a couple starts their life together, we doubt they expect their union to be unhappy or even ordinary. On the contrary, if any couple is asked what type of relationship they intend to have, they will usually say theirs will be among the greatest of all. Unfortunately, this goal of greatness is elusive to most people because they don't know how to go about becoming a team, even though at the beginning they may share love in abundance.

A Fish Story

You may have heard this aphorism: "Give a man a fish and you have fed him for a day. Teach a man to fish and you have fed him for a lifetime." Our book is about how to fish—in other words, guidance in the form of the attitudes and groundwork for achieving a close relationship. The specific details of how you achieve your goals is up to you because, as you study this book, you will become empowered to accomplish what all couples hope for.

Becoming a LoveTeam will depend upon the two of you working together to determine couple-specific goals. You'll also need to decide how to reach these goals. All decisions made should be based on your main team goals. We will help you through this process.

Think of an athletic team winning the state championship. It's never luck that allows them to accomplish this pinnacle of success. A marching band doesn't win a competition award by chance, nor does a company team reach their business goals by happenstance. Similarly, great relationships don't just happen either. It's necessary to have goals, as well as general and specific plans for achieving this success.

The goal of becoming a LoveTeam is new. Therefore, how to carry out *The LoveTeam Game Plan* will be given in enough detail throughout the book so it's clearly understood. The plan, again, *is for a loving couple to think, speak, and act like a team.*

The idea of team doesn't appear to be present in many committed relationships (yet), but it is part of the answer for a successful LoveTeam partnership. The other part is the element of love, which is not a typical aspect of most teams, such as those in corporations or athletics. None of these teams will ever have, nor should they have, the power and strength of a LoveTeam.

As you work at developing the right attitudes, habits, and other factors that will be explained, growth may be slow at first. But be encouraged; know that you are in the process of meeting your goals. Your effort together should be applauded and will soon bring long-term success when you're determined and committed.

A Hockey Miracle

Since 1964, our US Olympic team had been unsuccessful in beating the Russians in the Olympic games, as had all other teams. As success in anything is achieved by setting and working toward goals, having the right attitudes, and applying foundational skills, these and other team ideas defined the 1980 hockey team. The coach changed the way the team trained and played. In the end, they achieved what was considered a miracle by many—winning the gold medal!

Most people come into their relationship with a limited knowledge or desire to be a team player. In fact, many couples may be like an elementary student just learning to play basketball—excited to participate but bogged down by learning the rules and fundamentals. Or they may be more advanced, like a high school student who has already developed more of the basic attitudes and skills of the game, and now wants to be the best he or she can be. Seldom will both partners begin at the same level. Understanding this, even good couple relationships can become better with this LoveTeam approach.

When lovemates can see the benefits of thinking, acting, and making decisions based on being on the same team rather than as two individuals, they will never go back to their old system. Every direction of their lives would point toward responding and treating each other like a loving teammate.

The Challenge

When together or apart, much of what we think or say or do should revolve around this underlying question: "How can I help our team?" That idea can then be put into action and become part of a process that leads to developing positive habits and systems. This frame of mind would certainly lead to other questions we would ask ourselves as we go through each day, such as: "If this outside influence was allowed in, would our team become stronger?" Or, "Would doing or saying a certain thing benefit the relationship we're building together?"

Asking these types of questions is a proactive way for a lovemate to *anticipate* how they can help their team to become better. Also, it speaks volumes in showing their partner that they care. This caring attitude can be shown in small ways like noticing they need an extra hug, or in big ways like being there when they get a cancer diagnosis, and everything in between.

When a couple has grasped the LoveTeam concept, the love they have will carry them through times when one or both occasionally fall short as a teammate. The reverse is also true:

When they don't feel loving at times, knowing that their mate will be there for them restores the love.

As time goes on, relationships keep going in one direction, gradually getting better or getting worse. If your relationship is continuing to go in a downward direction, you know that changes need to be made. Becoming a LoveTeam is definitely a positive change. On a 1–10 scale (with 10 being best), if you have been, for example, a 0–2 in any of the team or love concepts and you change to even just a 3 in that area, you will change the dynamics and improve your team significantly. But why not aim high in each of the 24 aspects of LoveTeam that you'll read about here?

If a couple has *The LoveTeam Game Plan* that we're suggesting from Day One of their union and live it, there's no doubt that their relationship will be close, blissful, and fun. It is, however, more challenging to blend together team and love when both of these concepts are not nurtured from the beginning. Nevertheless, it's not only possible, but very likely that even a more "seasoned" couple will succeed when they persevere in putting this knowledge into practice on a daily basis. Are you ready for the challenge?

All You Need is Love—NOT!

It is said that love is all you need. And much is written about how to keep the love light burning bright, asserting that a strong love will carry any couple through everything. Really? This is not what we are seeing in our society today. Unfortunately, most relationship experts don't teach or write about team concepts. So the typical partnership doesn't have this extra element of team, at least not intentionally. To assume love is all that is needed is wrong because it's only part of what is necessary for a couple to grow and become all that they desire.

Many people say they "fell out of love" when their relationship gradually diminished, realizing that the love they had at the beginning faded. Adversity or unsolved problems leading to conflict had eaten away at their unity. Most likely what really happened is that they didn't understand and apply team principles. If they had, they would have naturally pulled together when adversity struck and avoided many of their problems in the first place.

John Ruskin, a prominent social thinker of the Nineteenth Century, said, "When love and skill [team] work together, expect a masterpiece." The combination of love and team in equal parts can be so much stronger than any other type of team, including athletic or business teams. Additionally, romantic feelings can flourish when the principles that make a team successful are applied in a committed partnership.

Sadly, in most cases, the intense emotional feelings of romance that couples experience when they are in the "honeymoon" period of their relationship only last less than three years, according to experts.[2] But we guarantee this doesn't have to be the case! These early feelings that are so wonderful and powerful can be continued throughout a relationship, no matter how long a couple is together.

Yes, love is great, awesome, fun, and necessary—but it's not enough by itself, as history has proven in too many cases. Unfortunately, most couples have been led to believe that love alone should be enough to manage all situations. In reality, what they lack is being committed teammates. If they've developed both factors of love *and* teamwork, then when the inevitable challenges and hardships of life arise, they will naturally turn to each other and draw closer instead of pulling apart.

One of the major purposes for developing a strong relationship is so that we become united in providing the support, affection, and compassion needed during times of adversity. How comforting to know we will have a loyal, understanding best friend by our side through the difficult times. Because we can't predict most tragedies or crises, it's vital to be proactively strong together before these occurrences happen. When this strength is present within a couple, then they can reach out together and provide empathy and support for others who face adversities in their lives.

An upcoming chapter, "The Snapshots," should encourage and motivate you to want more out of your relationship. As you read through the next few pages, we are certain you'll want to renew your goal to have a great partnership and adopt *The LoveTeam Game Plan* into your lives. The idea *for a loving couple to think, speak, and act like a team* will become an integral part of your lives. When you do this, you will become what most people only dream of—a great LoveTeam, with all of the wonderful benefits and advantages.

Chapter 1
Snapshots of a LoveTeam

XOXO

*Let the wife make the husband glad to come home,
and let him make her sorry to see him leave.*

~Martin Luther

What's the reason for any team to exist, including a LoveTeam? The answer is to deliver positive results. And what are the results of a great relationship? "The Snapshots" opens a window into what a joyful and fulfilling life together can look like for you, and for others who might observe you. As you read the next few pages of mental pictures, you'll realize they are examples of what couples experience when they have loving feelings toward each other and enjoy being on the same team.

"The Snapshots" on the next few pages are a guide, not an end product. They are just an overview of how a great partnership might look. You can use them as possible objectives, but are not necessarily given to be used as specific goals.

We don't think every couple has to do *all* of "The Snapshots." However, you may appreciate what it would be like to experience many of these ideas as part of your relationship. In fact, you will, no doubt, incorporate many of your own "Snapshots" as you learn about becoming a LoveTeam.

You may want to use "The Snapshots" as a "before" and "after" checklist. A 0–10 rating could be used (with 10 being best), with a suggestion that you rate your team now and along the way as you implement *The LoveTeam Game Plan* into your relationship.

When a couple starts this process, it can be comparable to taking a road trip to the Grand Canyon. You've never been there before, but have heard how awesome it is. You look on a map and it doesn't look like much of a challenge to get there—just a series of highways. You get on the road and discover that you have to cross over several high mountain passes, wait for a flood to recede, and change a flat tire, none of which you anticipated.

But you finally reach the rim of the breathtaking and majestic Grand Canyon—one of the natural wonders of the world! Was it worth the challenges you encountered to see all the wonders and beauty? To some it would be; to others, they would rather have stayed in their comfortable home. Even though you should expect to work and make changes, we hope "The Snapshots" will excite you to take the journey ahead and motivate you to stay on the road.

Chapter 2

"The Snapshots"

Team
We have made a commitment to each other.
We share and appreciate triumphs together.
Our weaknesses are complemented by our teammate's strengths.
We share our dreams, goals, desires, and hopes for the future.
We have a teammate for sharing tennis, board games, table tennis, and other games.
A positive attitude guides our relationship.
Together we support and encourage the activities of our family and friends.
We only speak positively to others about each other.
Our lovemate may complete us in doing things we can't or don't like to do.
We encourage the personal growth and development of our team and each other.
We build each other's confidence because we believe in each other.
In priorities and time, we become more disciplined and accountable.

We are each other's back-up plan.
We are great dance partners.
We know each other very well, and still like each other!
We celebrate birthdays, special occasions, and holidays together.
We enjoy sharing our meals.
Together we attend spectator sports, concerts, and so on.
We are comfortable in public with our teammate in conversation and actions.
We laugh at each other's jokes, whether funny or not.
Potential problems are discussed and solved as a team.
We make our first priority our team relationship.

Love
We give and receive unconditional love.
We share sexual intimacy.
We treat each other with respect, kindness, admiration, and courtesy.
We feel cherished and deeply appreciated.
A Saturday night date is guaranteed!
We enjoy the beauty in nature together—a sunset, the birds, and the bees!
We surprise each other with gifts, flowers, lunch box notes, cookies, and so on.
We kiss, hug, and cuddle daily.
We hold hands when taking a walk and other times.
We are in each other's loving thoughts much of the time.
We share romance.
We are best friends and companions.
We enjoy spending as much time together as possible.
Suggestions and input for improvement are lovingly given and received.
Our religious/spiritual life is shared.
Our need for touch (skin hunger) is satisfied.

We rub sore muscles and scratch itchy backs.
When one is emotionally down, the other lifts them up.
We lovingly motivate each other.
We laugh and enjoy our humor together.
We become better human beings—more tolerant, patient, and unselfish.
We have joy and happiness.

Team and Love

We accept each other's idiosyncrasies (unusual mannerisms).
We give to each other, expecting nothing in return.
We keep our secrets safe from other people.
We keep our relationship confidential.
Two heads are better than one in cooperative decision making.
We make uncomfortable situations comfortable for the other whenever possible.
We have happy memories.
We enjoy our vacations and outings.
The responsibility for raising our children is equally shared.
We participate in sports and outdoor adventures together.
We draw closer during and after adversity.
We provide a safe haven for each other from life's challenges.
We live longer lives.
We are each other's caregiver.
We are healthier.
We talk regularly to communicate our thoughts and concerns.
We physically and emotionally protect each other.
Together we establish family traditions.
We save each other from embarrassments (bad breath, mustard on clothes, etc.)
We can be the second person necessary in a project (a helper).
Household chores are shared as appropriate.
We are more successful in other areas of our lives.

We build our lives together.
Fun is part of our everyday lives!
We leave a lasting legacy for our children.
We are an example to others.

Chapter 3
A Wonderful Example

XOXO

Example is not the main thing in influencing others—it is the only thing.
~Albert Schweitzer

If you were asked, "Who is your role model?" what would you answer? If your parents were a positive influence in your life, you might simply answer the question without much thought and name both or either parent. If your parents were bad role models, you would quickly consider other people in your life to find an answer to that question. Certain people who have had bad role models will either decide to follow those examples or will decide to live their life acting differently, possibly even doing the opposite. We all can learn to be a good example no matter what our role modeling has been.

Throughout history, many children have wanted to follow in their parents' footsteps. If their parent was a scientist whom others admired, they also might want to become a scientist. They are more likely to become a volunteer if their parents were involved in volunteer activities. Or, if one of their parents was an alumni of a certain college or art institute, they may have a desire to attend that school as well. Hopefully, with good role models, our children will live their lives in a productive and responsible manner.

Legacy

As a couple lives out their everyday routines, they are ongoing examples of what they think of their commitments, and how highly they value their mate and their relationship. To put it concisely, they're on display. If they have children and grandchildren, they have an opportunity to pass down to them positive and motivating values of a committed partnership.

Some of the habits and attitudes children notice in their parents' relationship are when they watch them:

- Refer to things they have in common as "ours," instead of "mine"
- Treat each other with respect and courtesy
- Encourage and compliment each other
- Enjoy having fun together
- Spend their leisure time together, sharing most hobbies and interests
- Show affection
- Make decisions together
- Share household chores
- Hold hands when walking
- Seem to be best friends

When a child sees their parents having a great time together, they naturally look forward to their future when they also can have a wonderful relationship. Although good role models are not abundant (in fact, quite the opposite is true almost everywhere we look in our society), fortunate children know great relationships do exist. They know this because a loving relationship unfolds on a daily basis in their own home.

The legacy of a LoveTeam can affect not only our children, but also many generations. How a couple treats each other, how they solve their differences, and how they draw close during adversity all make a huge impact on their posterity. Children are not taught moral values and how to form relationships by being told; they are impacted through example, by what they observe. They are impressed by close, happy couples—and they do notice. Please don't be a great example of a bad example!

What would you want to be said at your funeral? How would you want your family to remember you? Most people are not remembered for their worldly successes, their material possessions, or their intellectual achievements. They are remembered for the example they set in their relationships.

Courage and Determination

Imagine the difficulty the early explorers experienced cutting their way through the wilderness, trekking up and down mountains, and fording streams. Compare that to driving down a modern interstate highway. There really is no comparison. What a model of determination and courage those early explorers are to us.

Similarly, the LoveTeam approach is new territory. It's not something that has ever been described in written form in this much detail. Courage and determination will be needed to model a great relationship in the society in which we live where the individual is prized so highly, marriage is the brunt of so many jokes, and those who value their relationship are often shunned. Think of yourself as an early explorer as you embark on the road to becoming a LoveTeam.

As we've traveled around the country, a few people we've encountered have been curious in a positive way when they see us holding hands and having a great time together. Some comments we have heard are, "Are you newlyweds?" "You're such a cute couple," and "You two are so lovey-dovey." We get many smiles as we hike hand-in-hand. In fact, as we walk near other couples, sometimes we see them take each other's hand and grin. It's contagious!

Once we went to a doctor's appointment, after not having been there for over a year. The receptionist commented, "I remember you two." When we asked her how she could remember us after so long, she replied, "Because you're the couple who are always holding hands." Little acts of closeness are noticed.

When the concepts in this book are learned and you begin to apply them, at first they may not seem very comfortable but soon will feel natural. If couples genuinely model a positive example of unity, our society would surely gain much. There would be a domino effect: less depression, more well-adjusted children, less crime, and the list goes on and on.

Couples can and will have an impact on so many people. Their examples will be felt not only by their children, but also their friends, relatives, neighbors, coworkers, and almost anyone with whom they come in contact. In our society, most committed couples keep their closeness to themselves—they may be embarrassed to show appropriate affection in front of others for fear of being shunned. Perhaps this is because they think other people might be sad or envious that they don't have this type of relationship. For the sake of our country, but especially for the young people in our society, it's our responsibility to counter the negativity about marriage we see in much of the media, government, corporate world, and other areas.

In almost any field, whether in athletics, science, business or the arts, people want to emulate success when they see it. Great people, companies, and teams inspire us. What a wonderful world it would be if close committed relationships were valued above any other successful endeavor or institution!

Part Two

The Power of Team

xoxo

Build for your team a feeling of oneness, of dependence on one another, and of strength to be derived by unity.

~Vince Lombardi

A book about teams and relationships—how can these two concepts possibly have anything in common? The word "team" conjures up many different images: a football stadium filled with boisterous fans cheering their team to victory; six employees sitting around a conference table discussing business tactics; Navy SEALS deciding their strategy for a dangerous mission. How do any of these situations possibly relate to couples?

In reality, every one of the above examples have team characteristics that are directly comparable to a personal relationship. The same factors that make a sports, business, or military team successful will also enable a couple to achieve the best that life has to offer.

Let's look at a doubles tennis team. Two people come together with comparable desires to play and be successful at tennis. But before that, they had to find a partner to begin the process of becoming a team. "Ditto"—we need someone to be part of our LoveTeam.

The tennis duo begins to practice using proven information given to them by coaches and others. They practice and do exercises that are known to bring success to a tennis team that wants to win. How successful they become depends on several aspects: If they have the right team spirit, if they're coachable, how well they integrate the approved techniques, and how hard they work, among others. "Ditto" for lovemates.

Unfortunately, there hasn't been a tried-and-true, proven method for couples to thrive. No one so far has written a manual using the same principles that have proven to be successful with *other* kinds of teams. If anything had been effective, one indicator would be a decreasing divorce rate. *Because this book is based on proven team-building principles,* it will empower you to be successful!

It's well known in the sports world that the most successful teams are the ones that integrate proven team concepts the most. The methods used by winning sports teams, and any other teams, are also true for a couple's relationship. When you add the equally important "Power of Love" described in Part Three, your success will be assured.

There are some relationship books on the market that suggest using team concepts, but none of them describe how this is to be done. We'll describe the necessary detail so as to be very understandable to everyone, even those who don't have a team background. Part Two will also show you the workings of high-functioning teams and relate this information to couples. But first, here's some necessary information about teams.

Establish Your Team

What's the difference between a team and a group? A team is defined as two or more people who work together toward the *same goal*, and are *interdependent* on each other to reach this goal.

A group, on the other hand, is two or more people with their own individual agendas and without a common purpose. They work mostly independently of each other. In addition, they lack common goals, mutual values, and shared responsibilities.

Examples of a group include people at an amusement park waiting to get on a ride, the sophomore class of a college, and passengers on an airplane. It's interesting that a group can quickly become a team if those involved develop a shared goal and have enough motivation to work closely together. Unfortunately, the reverse is also true: a team can become a group if members don't work together, lose their common goals, and aren't motivated to maintain their team status.

There is great diversity in teams. Certain teams are extremely close in their relationships and emotions, but others assemble only for a short time to get one job done. There are teams that come together for as little as an hour, and others that are together for years. Some examples of teams that can benefit society when they are successful are: hospital department employees, an Air Force squadron, a theater troupe, a construction team, a local school board, and an organization's budget committee. From this list, it's obvious that teams are varied and abundant, as well as being important in the functioning of our society.

Sadly, many couples still think of themselves as individuals instead of as an interdependent team with common goals. At one time or another most people have been on a team, unless they became a hermit at an early age! So, by using this beginning team experience, you can expand on that knowledge by studying this book and learning how your LoveTeam can be established. Then you can apply this exciting information to becoming a successful, high-functioning partnership.

Teamwork Works

James Bishop and K. Dow Scott write, "The use of work teams has been on the rise. Recent data indicate 47 percent of Fortune 1000 companies use teams to some extent, and 60 percent plan to increase the use of teams in the near future."[3]

Teamwork in large corporations has been around since the 1920s, but wasn't well understood until much later.[4] Many companies are turning to teamwork to breathe new life into old management styles. These older styles didn't work well because they emphasized and relied upon individuals working independently. Team-oriented companies have found that using team concepts leads to increased productivity, employee empowerment, and improved profits for the company.

Since teamwork is the answer for success in organizations, it's obviously also the answer for developing a team as permanent and all-encompassing as a committed couple. A word of caution, though: Either or both partners may be experiencing more team camaraderie in their workplace, with other people, or in outside interests than they are in their couple relationship. These other teams may compete with the couple's priorities. This is especially true when the other team has an uplifting, positive, cooperative environment and at home they don't have that. Thus, it's even more important to become a strong LoveTeam with each other.

The team system has been effectively used in athletics for well over 150 years. John Wooden, winning coach of eleven NCAA basketball championships and eighty-eight consecutive victories, devised the Pyramid of Success chart.[5] He recruited only men who would fit into his expectations of team players as defined by the chart, knowing that each player's attitudes and abilities would reflect on the team. In the same way, we originally chose our mate as someone who would fit our expectations. And they chose us for the same reasons. When we were dating, their *team spirit* was one of the characteristics we may have liked about them.

The Spirit of Team

Coach Wooden defined team spirit as "an eagerness to sacrifice personal interests and glory for the good and greatness of the team."[6] On any type of successful team, this spirit is what motivates, uplifts and makes us want to do better. "Never give up!" permeates every part of our attitude. Those with this spirit have enthusiasm, give encouragement and radiate a positive mood. Because people around them are uplifted and invigorated, it's a confidence builder.

Jennie Kakkad, a free-lance writer, says this about building team spirit:

> Team spirit is one of the essential agents to performance and success...The most important aspect of sharing a common goal is building a team spirit. Team spirit is a feeling of working together as one. Team spirit is the only ladder that can take any business to pride, expansion, and success. This emotional connection of the working group provides a deep sense of making a whole lot [of] difference through meaningful work.
>
> With the thought of "unity is strength," every big and small company is promoting team spirit as a part of their culture to pave [the] way to win the game...
>
> Encourage universal cooperation among team members...Give autonomy to the team and keep everything as simple as possible...Develop a healthy environment

by promoting humor and entertainment sessions [which] can help release tensions and improve the power of determination...Recognize and celebrate all the significant activities and milestones reached.

Kakkad also suggests having a "positive attitude with a feeling of we will win."[7]

It's not only a good idea to have the right kind of team spirit in our relationship, it is vital. So the first section of Part Two is devoted to Team Spirit.

A New and Improved Way

The power and scope of how the concept of team works in a couple relationship hasn't previously been realized. So new couples have been like inexperienced athletes. They start playing a game their first day without the teaching and applying of basic fundamentals, and no game plan or goals. This results in little or no improvement in skills or teamwork. There may be some couples who, early on, were fortunate in having good team role models or who instinctively applied team concepts. But more frequently this isn't the case.

In the sports world, when a person tries out and makes the team, they would have already developed certain individual athletic attitudes and skills desirable for the sport. When dating, the person we're dating will most likely want to continue our relationship if we've already developed certain personal characteristics that they're looking for.

In athletics, after they make the team, players help their new team to develop strategies in becoming well-balanced and successful. Similarly, after a couple becomes committed, ideally the two of them work together to mutually cooperate and complete each other so that they, too, are well-balanced and successful. Since history has shown that this isn't the case in many relationships, the detailed information in this book should be very helpful.

Some Differences

Even though there are many similarities between sports or business teams and LoveTeams, there are also some differences. Most other teams are out to be better than their competition; they show aggressiveness, and compete to win, sometimes at any cost. Instead of being aggressive, couples have affection, romance, and love, all of which will be discussed in Part Three. Additionally, they don't try to "beat" any other teams or people, so there's no thought of winning or losing.

Another difference between a LoveTeam and most other teams is that the athlete or corporate employee has a manager, coach, or supervisor to whom the team reports. However, a couple is *self-managed*. They equally live, work, and play together to develop their relationship and cooperatively make decisions. Examples of other self-managed teams include a business partnership, a skating pair, and a two-person comedy act.

Most teams keep score and may keep statistics about each player's personal achievements. However, there should be no scorekeeping in a partnership—no adding up what one does good or bad compared to the other. In fact, scorekeeping, in the traditional sense of the word, is usually detrimental to a relationship.

Life is Better

As in any successful endeavor, there should be a combination of work and fun. Being on a team isn't all drudgery, practice, and hard work, or few would be motivated to stay on the team. The more successful teammates get at developing their team, the more closeness and fun they experience.

Similarly, when a LoveTeam is more stable and mature, life is so much more fulfilling and exciting. Since we spend more time with each other than with any other team we might be on, it should be clear how being lovemates can be so much better.

This Part is divided into three sections: Team Spirit, Team Fundamentals, and Team Completion. Since these are new ideas for relationships, we'll describe in the upcoming twelve chapters each important concept in detail and give many examples. Team Spirit is about attitude and mental outlook. The basics of healthy team methods are explained in Team Fundamentals. The four chapters of Team Completion describe how differences can actually be used to a partnership's advantage.

We believe that every couple is instinctively familiar with the concepts of team already because some of them were surely present when they were dating. Integrating these ideas more extensively back into your relationship, as well as other unfamiliar ones you'll be shown, will restore the fascination and excitement you experienced early on, except with even more depth and feeling. If an athletic team is willing to do for a season what it takes to be a successful team, wouldn't you be willing to do what it takes since it's for a lifetime?

xoxo
Team Spirit

Chapter 4

We Not Me

XOXO

One man can be a crucial ingredient on a team, but one man cannot make a team.

~Kareem Abdul-Jabbar

When a sports star is interviewed after a winning game, they almost always give credit to their team for the win, not any one thing they personally did. Also, a team player seldom comments, on or off the field, about a particular teammate's mistake made in the game. This spirit of team-like thinking is key in the making of successful sports teams, as well as in great relationships.

You'll see that instead of using terms like *I* or *my* or *mine*, it's beneficial to the development of your team to form the habit of using the pronouns *we* or *our* or *ours*. It will be amazing how just this little change of habit will help you both think more as team members and less as individuals. As a result, you'll feel a special closeness with each other.

Movin' On

When they're planning to get married, many people expect that their lifestyle won't change much after they marry. If they're firm about this expectation, then their thinking may not be conducive to marital success—it wouldn't be fair to their spouse. Ideally, both husband and wife should be focused on the goal of making their union strong. Forming habits and patterns that unite the two will, in time, become more natural. Unselfishness and teamwork are major elements that enhance a marriage and enable a couple to grow into a very close LoveTeam.

When life's circumstances change, we need to adjust to the changes. For example, newly widowed individuals are lovingly advised by grief counselors that in a short, reasonable time after their spouse dies they should begin to think in terms of *I* instead of *we*, otherwise they can't move on in life. Of course this doesn't happen overnight—it takes time—but the grieving process will be prolonged until the person accepts that they're now single.

As with the recently widowed person, newlyweds should accept that their status in life has changed, but in a wonderful way! When they embrace this change, they'll have a smoother transition into marriage, and the adjustments that are inevitable will not be difficult. The engagement period is the ideal time to make the transition from *me* to *we*. However, it certainly can still be done at any stage in a marital partnership. It just takes a change in attitude and a conscious effort.

Roommates or Lovemates?

On elementary school basketball teams, usually the coach encourages the players to pass the ball several times before shooting. In this way, one person won't take all the glory for shooting the basket. Instead, each player learns to also utilize the attributes and skills of their teammates. However, because some children are immature in their social skills, they'll often revert to selfish ways during a game and shoot without passing.

Similarly, couples often revert to their single ways, when each of them did what they wanted to do and when they wanted to do it. This includes their own interests, friends, vacations, habits, and activities. They become little more than roommates instead of lovemates. If one is thinking interdependently but the other isn't, there can only be, at best, a mediocre relationship. Unfortunately, the team-oriented one may in time become disheartened and begin to prioritize other people, places, and things. This leads to living separate lives.

Our society tells us to take care of ourselves before anyone else: "Do your own thing." "If you don't take care of yourself, no one else will." "Think of yourself first." In a great relationship, both individuals have a mature attitude. According to Dr. John A. Schindler, MD, in his book *How to Live 365 Days a Year*, a mature attitude includes unselfishness, flexibility, and adaptability.[8] He writes:

> Maturities are, after all, nothing more than certain definite attitudes we develop in regard to ourselves and our relation to our world. But they are attitudes that are not developed without learning processes. They do not come naturally to people. They are part of the things we must learn. These attitudes determine whether we live happily or unhappily.[9]

It takes time and consideration to develop habits that are team oriented. For example, when bringing in groceries together, one person willingly walks to the far end of the kitchen counter to put their bags down in order to leave space at the close end for the other's bags. The first doesn't think twice about taking a few extra steps, knowing their actions make it easier for the other.

"Who do you play for?"

We suggest that couples watch the movie *Miracle*[10] to see how individuals came together to form a very successful team that won the gold medal in ice hockey at the 1980 Winter Olympics. In one scene at the beginning of their training, the coach asked the players, "Who do you play for?" One by one, the answer each typically gave was the college they had attended. In a later scene, when they weren't performing well as a team, the coach made them skate back and forth across the ice many times until they were exhausted, while he continued directing them, "Again." "Again." "Again," after each lap. Finally, one player said, "I play for the United States of America," instead of the name of his college. At that moment the coach excused the team. They had finally gotten the point that they were now part of this new Olympic team.

It may be okay to pursue an individual activity or interest as long as both partners have discussed the situation completely and they agree. Most importantly, the team shouldn't be negatively impacted by the decision.

When we're talking about anything that affects both of us we should include our mate, *even when they're not present*. Most topics do—our children, our home, our belongings, our vacation, our joint decisions. Of course, there are certain things we do individually which we refer to singly, such as *my* job or *my* doctor. But whenever there's anything we have in common, it helps us think interdependently if we refer to those things as *ours*.

Even when we're not physically with our lovemate, we should still be aware of our team relationship and be loyal to our joint decisions. For example, if one partner needs to work late and they've agreed ahead of time how they'll handle such a situation, they should do what has been agreed upon. In other words, they prioritize their mate, their team relationship, and the decisions they've made together.

If you are standing next to a business associate who's on your team at work and you both are speaking to a third party, would you refer to your team as "my team," or as "our team"? Saying "our team" would give the correct impression that the coworker on your team is an appreciated member whom you value. This is a *we not me* mentality.

One way to strengthen team spirit is to have a shared identity. When we do or say something that creates this identity with the other, it's quite a compliment to them. Couple identity is obvious when we have pictures of us together around our home and at our workplace. Athletic teams show oneness and pride in their team by wearing the same uniforms. Couples could wear matching or similar leisure clothing, such as t-shirts or hats, that show each is proud to be connected.

If both are team players, their relationship has a much improved chance of being awesome because they're thinking interdependently—*we not me*. We should tell and show the other that we're proud to be associated with them and happy to be their lovemate. Indeed, we know how good it makes us feel when someone acts proud and happy to be associated with us!

Chapter 5

Do and Be Our Best

XOXO

Great effort springs naturally from great attitude.
~Coach Pat Riley

John Wooden, one of the most successful college basketball coaches of all time, writes, "Success is peace of mind which is a direct result of self-satisfaction in knowing you did your best to become the best that you are capable of becoming."[11] There's a "best" way of doing anything. In baseball, for a batter there's a best stance, a best swing, and a best follow-through. When cooking there's a certain order to add ingredients so that the recipe comes out the tastiest. When getting a bill through Congress, there's a best way of following procedures to make sure it passes.

There are ways of doing and saying things that will build our relationship. And to do so we may have to get out of our individual comfort zone. It usually isn't a plus to say, "But I've always done it this way," or "That's just the way I am." When we make improvements for the betterment of our relationship, it will increase our chances of becoming closer.

You Won the Prize

When dating, people put their best foot forward. On an athletic team, people do their very best when they try out for the team. In business, in order to be hired we're at our best through the interviewing process.

After we become committed to our relationship, make the team, or get hired, we shouldn't sit back and glory in the fact that we've made it. To be a teammate who helps the organization be successful, we stay motivated and work to help the team improve. We want to continue to be our best, whether it's in our chosen sport, in our job, or any team we're on. So to become the best LoveTeam possible, we give our all and focus much of our time and energy on building our team.

As a single individual, a person may just strive to attain average goals, which is all right since they aren't affecting anyone else. A singles tennis player can play to have fun and get some exercise without setting competitive goals. But when we play doubles tennis, someone else is now depending on us to do our best—to put in a great effort. If a person starts their own business, average goals are okay. But if they take in a partner or hire any employees, then their work ethics and goals should reflect the team.

Similarly, when we're a couple, we have a teammate who needs us to be our best—who may want to follow *The LoveTeam Game Plan*. They may truly want to have a great relationship, but they can't do it by themselves. So if we don't do our best, we're letting our team down and disappointing our mate.

There's a saying that goes, "A winner says, 'I'm good, but not as good as I want to be.' A loser says, 'I'm not as bad as a lot of other people.'" In sports, teams usually have three possible goals: To win, to do their best, or to just have fun. Another option for some teams is to not even show up; in other words, they forfeit.

To relate the above four possible goals or options to our relationship, there's a correlation to winning when couples set a good example for their children, their grandchildren, and others to follow. When they do their best, they are motivated to improve and be successful, thus their partnership will be joyful through the years. If we're together only to have fun—we don't exert much time or effort—our team won't improve, which ultimately won't be fun. A forfeiture is where the couple communicates very little and they live mostly separate lives.

Consideration

Partners in a LoveTeam consistently discuss and work on their goals, their plan to reach those goals, household chores, careers, parenting, recreational activities, vacations, celebrations—everything. This is not a surface relationship. It's fun, but it's also work. And anything that's worthwhile is worth exerting great effort, our best effort. Good news: As time goes on and healthy relationship habits are established, gradually it becomes less work and more fun. (See Chapter 10, "Healthy Habits are Vital")

For a great relationship to develop, we should be the best we can be by considering what will be good for the other person. Thus, as any good teammate would do, we should be motivated to improve our weaknesses, such as becoming more patient. And we build on our strengths as well, such as organizational skills. It's also important to get to know our mate more completely and analyze how we can be the best possible for him or her, thus completing their character traits.

Relationships are much more about *being* the right person rather than *having* the right person. Being a considerate teammate should be a very high concern. Here are a few examples:

- If our partner is waiting for us to do something or go somewhere, we shouldn't make them wait or have to come and get us.
- Drive so that we make them, not necessarily us, comfortable in the car.
- Take the time to plan meals we know our mate enjoys.
- When in a group, avoid drawing attention if we know it would embarrass our lovemate.
- Be attentive to how we present ourselves to others when we're together.

There are many other ways we can show each other consideration and give them the attention they deserve. It's not easy to do; it takes putting ourselves in their place and imagining how we would feel if we were them.

Challenge Yourselves

In basketball, players usually learn to dribble with only one hand. To be their best, they challenge themselves to not only dribble with their right *and* left hands, but also to dribble between their legs! In relationships, we could give ourselves a somewhat similar challenge as well. If we really want to excel, we should go beyond the usual habits and attitudes and do our best in situations that aren't the norm. For example, we could reduce our partner's stress when they've had a bad day, be affectionate when they're being grumpy, and forgive them even when they don't apologize.

In athletic games, competition is a major motivator for doing one's best. Emotions can run very high during intense events.

However, there's a big difference between personal relationships and athletics. Those same emotions can drive a wedge between the two if they become too competitive with each other. We want to be on each other's side—not be their competitor.

In their relationships, most people don't think in terms of doing their very best. However, partnerships don't stay the same over the years—they go either in an upward or a downward direction. When you give your best effort to every aspect of your twosome, you will always be winners. You won the "prize," now show your teammate that you value them as a prize, and that you will accept the challenge to help your LoveTeam be great!

Chapter 6
An Optimistic Attitude

XOXO

*Positive thinking will let you do everything
better than negative thinking will.*

~Zig Ziglar

Norman Vincent Peale, author of *The Power of Positive Thinking*, writes that an optimistic way of life "is wonderful. It is not easy. Indeed, it often is hard, but it is full of joy, hope and victory."[12] It's easier for some people to see the positive instead of the negative in most everything when they form the habit of doing so.

Martin Seligman, in his book *Authentic Happiness*, writes about a research study of a group of 180 nuns who wrote their short autobiographies just before they took their vows. The amount of positive feeling in their essays was quantified by raters in the study who didn't know how long the nuns lived. It "was discovered that 90 percent of the most cheerful quarter was alive at age eighty-five versus only 34 percent of the least cheerful quarter. Furthermore, 54 percent of the most cheerful quarter was alive at age ninety-four, as opposed to 11 percent of the least cheerful quarter."[13]

Likewise, 100,000 women were involved in The Women's Health Initiative, a study conducted by the United States government. Those rated optimistic were 14 percent less likely than pessimists to die during the study's first eight years.[14]

One quality that all successful athletic teams have in common is that they are positive. It's only possible to have a winning team when the players are positive because even one negative player may permeate the entire team in time. In the same way, it's only possible to have a great relationship if optimism is part of the foundation. What an advantage it is when both are optimistic!

Do You Think Positively?

Let's say someone asks you to drive to the next town, where you've previously never been. Does your mind quickly jump to the excitement of a new adventure awaiting you, or do you think first of the pitfalls that might ensue?

If you get ten wrong on a test, do you think of the ninety you answered correctly, or dwell on the ten you got wrong?

If your mate suggests attending a certain event together, do you initially think of pleasing them and how it should be fun, or do you first think of the reasons why you both shouldn't go?

When you have time to just relax and think, what do you think about the majority of the time? Do you think positive or negative thoughts? If they're about your lovemate, are your thoughts usually more positive or more negative?

Exercises in Optimism

One thing we can do as an exercise in positive thinking is to think back on some of the happy memories we've had that can be revisited mentally when necessary or desired. This can invigorate us by remembering upbeat experiences we've shared. Some examples include your wedding or honeymoon; a special time you planned for your partner, like a surprise party; the loving things they do for you; and when you pulled together through a difficult experience or time period, remembering how supportive they had been.

A heartfelt effort to think more about the present and plan for the future goes a long way in curbing the desire to remember the negatives of the past. In order to maintain a positive attitude, it's important to be able to move forward and not let a past issue dominate the present.

Another exercise is to think in terms of the half full cup. For example, when driving home from work, look forward to coming in the door and finding a cheerful lovemate greeting you at the door. That hasn't always been the case; sometimes you walked into a hornet's nest when you entered your home. Instead, think about all the times you came into a wonderful scenario.

We've found the following practice to be effective for us: When we don't feel like being positive, we still make ourselves think, say, or do a positive thing. For example, if you hear something on television and you're about to voice a negative comment, force yourself to say something good instead. As you "go through the motions" of being positive, you'll find that your mood will soon catch up with your actions. Additionally, if you find that you're immersed in negativity, it may be time to rethink your habits.

When either person feels anxious, it usually affects the relationship negatively because worrying doesn't lend itself to being loving and team-oriented. So when we have an anxious thought or moment, we can develop a habit of having a predetermined way to counter that feeling. For example, think of an uplifting quote you've previously memorized, sing a certain song that is bright and cheerful, or say or do something similar that will offset the anxiousness.

We should always think the best of our mate and first give them the benefit of any doubt, assuming they have a good reason for their words or actions. We can consciously adjust our mindset to be agreeable. If we both do this, there's no doubt that we'll have an improved quality of life together. Having a habit of first thinking favorably about their ideas and opinions allows us to arrive at a positive conclusion more often than not. As a result, we'll feel like we're on the same team and will both have more loving feelings. This will start a wonderful cycle of goodwill and closeness in our LoveTeam.

Minimize the Negative

There's a common belief that it takes up to twenty positives to offset one negative. A negative can be our words, our actions, or an outside influence. And, the more negatives a person experiences in a day, the more they have to work at being positive. So it becomes essential for a couple to minimize the negatives in their daily lives.

These occurrences may come from many directions, and most of them can be controlled. Outside negatives might include our living conditions, people who create stress, a driving commute, a job that's taxing, health problems, and even quarreling children. When we perceive that we're anxious or irritable from a particular source, we should brainstorm together to determine the best way to reduce the anxiety-provoking situation. Worrying is habit forming and almost always affects a relationship in a negative way. It is non-team and also non-loving. We can choose to stay calm and serene, which is much healthier for our relationship.

Another way to minimize the negative is to limit saying the word "no" when speaking to our mate. This can be with minor situations, or when no one really knows the answer. Rather than a curt "No," how much sweeter it is to answer something like, "I'm not sure, but it might be...," or "You could be right, but have you considered...?" These show a positive attitude toward and respect for our best friend. And, anyway, we might be wrong! After all, what's more important—that we're right or that we don't hurt our relationship?

Another habit that can cause irritation is when we correct our mate about trivial details that don't really matter. Is it worth the problems it could cause to clarify whether we were thirty or thirty-one years old when something happened? Or that a word should be pronounced a different way? Or that we were in one state or another when we had an experience while on vacation?

We'll all have negative things happen in our lives. Let's think of this adversity as a motivation to strengthen our character and our resolve, instead of as an excuse to be negative or unkind. Using positive LoveTeam concepts, we can bounce back quicker and better than ever from adversity.

Maximize the Positive

In professional baseball, one hit every three times at bat will put you on the All-Star team. The pessimist thinks, "I failed two times." The optimist looks at the success and excitement of the one hit.

In *The Art of Doubles,* Pat Blaskower explains: "All good doubles [tennis] teams communicate frequently...They share ideas, give positive and specific suggestions...[and] encourage one another... Both partners should communicate kindly, thoughtfully, positively, and confidently, even under the most adverse circumstances."[15]

When talking to each other, it helps to be positive, loving, and forgiving rather than adversarial, defensive, or critical. In addition, positivity leads to less stress, improved health, and a longer lifespan. That's a win/win for our relationship!

It's especially important to be positive concerning our mate when we're with other people, whether our teammate is present or not. Saying only positive and respectful comments about or to our partner when we're with others lets everyone know they are the most important person in our life. It shows how much we value them. They will appreciate our respect, and it also demonstrates our relationship at its best.

A study by two psychologists was done of 141 women whose picture appeared in a 1960 yearbook of Mills College in Oakland, California. All but three of the women were smiling, and half of the smilers had a "Duchenne smile." Guillaume Duchenne, a French neurologist, discovered a smile that's more genuine where the corners of the mouth turn up and the corners of the eyes crinkle, like crow's feet. The researchers wrote:

> All the women were contacted at ages twenty-seven, forty-three, and fifty-two and asked about their marriages and their life satisfaction… Astonishingly, Duchenne women, on average, were more likely to be married, to stay married, and to experience more personal well-being over the next thirty years. Those indicators of happiness were predicted by a mere crinkling of the eyes.[16]

A recent study at Harvard University showed that people who smile more are hired more often, get a higher percentage of promotions, and make more money.[17] It takes thirty-seven muscles to frown, but only twenty-two to smile.

If being positive isn't an easy habit at this point in your life, one thing that might help is to display quotes around your home or workplace about being positive, such as, "Most folks are as happy as they make up their minds to be." (Abraham Lincoln) Or "A pessimist sees the difficulty in every opportunity; an optimist sees the opportunity in every difficulty." (Winston Churchill)

Any person at any time can consciously begin to practice the wonderful art of positive thinking. As our thoughts become more positive, our words and actions will become uplifting and optimistic. This will have a direct effect on our relationship: it will improve and, as a result, life will be more joy-filled. Indeed, consistently utilizing positive thinking can be a life-changing experience, for us and for those around us.

Chapter 7

Support Without Regrets

XOXO

This is the team. We're trying to go to the moon. If you can't put someone up, please don't put them down.

~NASA motto

There are several types of fans at a sporting event. Some fans cheer only when the team is doing well. Others cheer both when the team is succeeding and when they're losing. These fans are encouraging when the team needs it the most—when they need support, an emotional lift, and motivation to do their best. When things are going well, it's nice for players to hear accolades. But it's critical when things aren't going well.

Similarly in our relationship, it's easy to be happy for and supportive of the other when they achieve or excel at a task. This is expected, comes naturally for most people and is important to do. But our partner also needs us when they're having a bad day, when they're disappointed about something, or when they're not feeling well. By our encouragement, they know that we're on their side, as with the second type of fans who show support when their team is down. Loyal fans and lovemates are always there for the other.

Our Biggest Fan

We've all heard of the phrase *home court advantage* as related to sports. The advantage isn't just because the team is familiar with their own court or field—it's also because they know their local cheerleaders and fans believe in them and have come to the game to show it. Because of all this encouragement, the team is more likely to succeed at home than on the road. Does your partnership have home court advantage?

We should be each other's biggest fan to keep our relationship going in an upward direction. So, we have our own built-in, one-person cheerleading squad. Lovemates mutually support and encourage each other by actively noticing and commenting on their partner's achievements, whether large or small. They freely give genuine compliments, even look for reasons to show appreciation. They should be as excited when the other does something well as if they had done it themselves. As the Three Musketeers would say, "All for one, one for all!"

When we give positive reinforcement, this acknowledges and encourages our companion's actions. Rabbi Zelig Pliskin writes about this in his book, *Marriage:*

> I once saw this advertisement: "Make sure you're part of a winning team." The way to be part of a winning team in marriage is to bring out the best in your spouse. Remember to keep your focus on your spouse's strengths and not his or her weaknesses. Remember to believe in the potential of your spouse. Believe that your spouse has untapped wisdom and goodness that both of you can reach. Remember to notice positive changes and to express your appreciation. Express appreciation and

gratitude for positive words and actions, even if they are not totally what you would have wanted. By giving positive reinforcement to a movement in the right direction, you encourage your spouse to keep moving along the best path for both of you.[18]

As Rabbi Pliskin has pointed out, when we receive words of support and encouragement from our teammate, we need to appreciate their appreciation!

A sports team supports and gives positive reinforcement to other members of their team. This motivates them to keep doing their best, and helps lift them up when they're having difficulty. This support continues during the entire season. Likewise, on a LoveTeam we need to support and encourage each other every day throughout our lives.

When a couple is going through adversity, it's especially important that they put their full effort into supporting each other. This may not be the time to reach out to others who may also be going through difficulty. The time to offer help to others will come later, when the couple's adversity is past and their relationship is strong. Family, friends, and others should support the couple during adversity, similar to loyal fans who support their athletic team. Sometimes this support by others is simply to respect the couple's need for privacy.

It's also true that when we're neutral about giving support, it's not uplifting for the other person. We may be thinking encouraging thoughts, but unless we voice them our mate won't feel our support. Likewise, encouragement that we give to our partner should be reciprocated to us when we need it.

Increased Attention
Everyone is different in his or her needs at stressful times and during adversity. Only by knowing the other very well can

we give them individualized attention. For instance, a person may need happy, loving, vocal encouragement at one particular time. Another time they may need respectful, silent support that allows them to just sit and think.

Raising our teammate's spirits when they're down is like the sports fans who give encouragement when their team isn't having success. When our mate is feeling defeated, we should increase our attention, love, and affection so that they feel our support and we don't have any regrets later on. Some examples include the loss of a promotion or job, when the dinner they prepared is burned, or when they're suffering with poor health.

We can also reassure our partner when they venture into uncharted territory. They may be unsure of themselves and lack confidence, really needing their loyal fan at such a time. A literature professor named John A. Holmes declared, "There is no exercise better for the heart than reaching down and lifting people up."

A Supportive Team

Usually one person in the relationship has more knowledge, background, or passion in a particular area, so assumes the leadership role. The other should be helpful, cooperative, and trusting when they work together in that area. Even if the leader makes a mistake, it's more important that, as the helper, we continue to show confidence in them. They'll remember our loving support, whether right or wrong. This isn't easy to do, but we'll feel their adoration when we do.

When playing a game or sport, it's best to be on the same team if possible. If it's just the two of us playing, the attitude should be one of friendly competition: cheering, complimenting, and boosting each other's morale. It's all about having fun together.

Sometimes there's more strength in non-verbal than verbal encouragement. For example, we should go to each other's doctor appointments together whenever possible. When meeting with the doctor, two heads are better than one in remembering what was said and the care instructions given. Additionally, the doctor will then know this patient has someone who cares. For a doctor this is important because statistically a patient with an advocate and a support system will be more compliant and often will have a better medical outcome.

Surround with Support

During the wedding ceremony, the officiator says to the audience something similar to this: "If anyone has any reason why this couple should not be joined, speak now or forever hold your peace." From the moment a couple is wed, the family and friends of the couple should give only encouragement and support; they shouldn't take sides, be negative toward either spouse, or give advice unless asked by the couple.

Likewise, this means we should be supportive and encouraging to the other couples in our lives—parents, adult children, and others. A married couple is the basic unit, or team, in our society and all other teams are secondary. Our society functions optimally when this basic unit is strengthened.

Imagine being at a high school football game and your team is losing in the first half. They come back after halftime and play like a completely different team, finally winning the game. You wonder what happened in the locker room. Did the coach's pep talk give them that extra burst of adrenalin, or did he employ another approach? All you know is they were much more motivated for the second half. The coach knows the team members and what it takes to make them successful.

Similarly, when one of us is having difficulty, to help our lovemate it may be best to first slow things down. In other words take a break, as the football team did at halftime. Then, because we know our teammate so well, we can give specialized encouragement, a pep talk so to speak, to help them through this difficult time and bring them out of their slump.

Our love and encouragement is so important in our relationship as everyone has disappointments, trials, and adversity. What an opportunity we have in the daily giving and receiving of this positive and uplifting type of support. We can live without regrets, and feel fortunate to have home court advantage every day.

xoxo
Team Fundamentals

Chapter 8
Basic Principles

XOXO

*Team energy multiplies when you set a
desired goal and resolve to achieve it.*

~Anonymous

A bad attitude by a player in sports won't only limit them personally, but will also have a negative effect on their team. Conversely, a great attitude by an athlete is essential for developing the proper fundamentals that are important in building any type of team, including a great relationship team. Now that you know how important it is to have the right team spirit and attitudes, you are ready to learn about the basic principles that are at the core of achieving a LoveTeam.

In *Shortcut Through Therapy*, Richard Carlson explains:

> To master anything, you need to understand the fundamental principles involved. Once you own the ideas, there's no need to keep discussing them... The

principles are the most relevant information; once you understand them, happiness comes right away.[19]

This is certainly true in a relationship. The strongest and most basic principle in determining whether you can be a great teammate for your partner is that *you decide to and are eager to be their teammate*. Hopefully both of you have, or will soon have, the attitude and the desire to develop into a stronger team. This chapter and the following three will clarify the basic principles.

A Solid Foundation

Think of a team of architects. One of their first considerations when planning a building is to be sure the blueprints include a solid foundation. Without this, no structure will endure very long. A minor earthquake has toppled many buildings that didn't have the proper support at the bottom.

When dating, many people are looking for rather superficial values in a mate: Are they good looking? Do they drive a nice car? Do they make a lot of money? These and other values that are also superficial will become less important as the relationship progresses. If similar traits are the main emphasis in choosing a mate, the couple may not have the proper support at their foundation. However long you've been in your relationship, what's important now is that you realize what the right principles are and change your thinking, if necessary, so that your union can become strong.

It's so nice when a person realizes their mate is excited about them, delighted to have them as a teammate. Knowing this usually motivates the other to improve anything about themselves that isn't helpful to their relationship. When both partners are moving in these directions, this can go a long way in making the partnership stable, secure, and satisfying.

It wouldn't be smart to allow someone with a jackhammer to come in and break up the concrete for a building's foundation after it's laid. To build a strong relational foundation, we should minimize or eliminate anyone or anything that doesn't support our team, or that may even tear it down.

Societal Norms

Our society isn't marriage friendly. For anyone wanting to have a great relationship today, there are some very important negative factors to be aware of. These standards have permeated many parts of our world, subconsciously infiltrating the thoughts and actions of many people and institutions. We believe they're detrimental to two people becoming a LoveTeam. Some of these societal norms include the following:

- There's a strong emphasis on the individual, even when they're committed or married, rather than on the partners as a unit.
- Couples are usually separated in many settings—men meet with men and women meet with women.
- Partners are often encouraged to give and receive their emotional support primarily from friends or relatives, rather than from their mates.
- The opposite gender is so different from us that we aren't compatible and can't understand each other.
- If a person has failed at one marriage, they will probably fail at another.
- We are told we should stay in our individual comfort zone, even when we're a couple.

Too often, just being in love has proven to be inadequate in overcoming these anti-team, non-unifying values. But with the addition of becoming a LoveTeam, a couple can thrive because they live team ideas and are united.

Think Team

It's very important to realize that each of us has complete control over our own thoughts. We choose the direction our words and actions take by what we think about and what we mentally decide to dwell on or let go.

Two people on a tandem bicycle form a team. They go in the same direction at the same speed, powered by both participants. If necessary, one can pedal while the other rests. The one behind has to trust the front partner to steer safely and correctly. But the one behind is also part of the decision-making process—where they go, how they get there, and when they stop. Either one can put the brakes on. Pedaling together, the two of them can go faster than just one and use less energy. In fact when they work together, they actually spur each other on.

What would be the consequences if the bicyclists couldn't agree on the route to take? Or one pedaled too slowly? It surely wouldn't be the pleasant outing they both envisioned when they planned the ride.

Teammates share responsibilities, consider the other's ideas, anticipate needs, and work to solve any differences of opinion. They do their best at every task, changing to improve if necessary, so that their LoveTeam can do well in a supportive atmosphere.

Own the Idea

As mentioned above, a major problem for personal relationships today is the emphasis society puts on individualism. As a result, many people think their mate prevents them from meeting their own individual needs and goals. These people obviously aren't thinking of their partner as their teammate.

A fundamental factor to having a great relationship is to not only accept that we're a couple, but to be grateful for it, and own the idea of being half of the team.

There's such a dramatic difference between the moment before we make a commitment to our partner and the moment after. For married couples, it's the moment we say "I do." A couple lifestyle is vastly different from single life. Therefore, it's imperative to not just reluctantly accept that fact, but thankfully enjoy the numerous benefits that a LoveTeam brings. (Refer to the chapter, "The Snapshots.") We think that a committed relationship, with its balance sheet of pluses and minuses, has many more advantages than single living.

Ask a person on a soccer team what they'd do if they were the only player on the team. Who would pass to them? Who would offer words of encouragement? And with whom would they celebrate their successes? Our relationship gives us similar opportunities and a myriad of others.

After learning what is fundamental for a successful union, couples will consciously need to go against the current prevailing values that weaken their relationship. When they do, great things can happen because two people have embraced the wonderful idea of being a LoveTeam, and are eager to be each other's teammate.

Chapter 9

Commitment and a Climate of Trust

XOXO

Every kind of peaceful cooperation among men is primarily based on mutual trust.
~ ALBERT EINSTEIN

On any team, it's vital for each team member to know that the other team members are in it for the long haul. Then they can trust that their teammates will hold up their part of the agreed-upon action plan. Vince Lombardi said, "Individual commitment to a group effort—that is what makes a team work, a company work, a society work, a civilization work." We confirm that this is part of what makes a relationship work as well.

When we're on any close-knit team, an act or attitude by one of our mates that's unteam-like hits us harder than if we were just a group of individuals. Everyone knows that when a team member doesn't live up to their commitment, it adversely affects all the others. This is especially profound in a partnership because there are only two people involved.

An Insurance Policy

When we're dating, commitment isn't a big issue. However, after the wedding, commitment becomes a huge issue. Our commitments determine how we respond to situations after we marry and how we decide to live our lives together. Our marriage vows should be like an insurance policy, committing us to a relationship much deeper and more satisfying than when we were just dating.

When you join an athletic team, you make a commitment for the season to be part of that team. As a player, you don't individually decide to change the game plan or the goals to which you previously agreed. This would be unethical, and your reliability as a teammate would be questioned.

Similarly, in many professions a person signs a contract with their new company, agreeing to meet certain professional standards and live by a code of conduct while employed there. Most employee contracts don't require a long-term time commitment. A marriage contract, however, does have a time commitment: "Until death do us part." We agreed to this when we married. Great news: the marriage contract has so many more advantages than any other contract we'll ever sign!

Team Commitment

A team of department store clerks work together to keep shelves stocked and answer customers' questions. Their responsibilities may include covering each other's breaks and helping out if a fellow team member needs assistance. There's give and take, each responding to the other's needs and getting the help they need in return. One day, one of the team clerks doesn't come to work and fails to notify the supervisor, who would have called in a replacement. This leaves the team short-handed for the day, resulting in complaints by customers, empty shelves, and a stressed-out team. The uncommitted employee has caused a breakdown in the team's trust. Because this lack of commitment in our society as a whole threatens relationships as well, a LoveTeam approach is the answer.

Commitment in general has changed over the last forty years. Most employees previously stayed with one job their entire working career. Now, only occasionally do employees stay with one company for longer than a few years. To reverse this expensive turnover trend, many employers are teaching a team approach to their work force. Shelley Frost of *Small Business Chron* writes, "Teamwork activities that focus on commitment bring staff members closer together with a greater sense of direction. Individual employees are able to see how their level of commitment affects their colleagues and your company's success."[20]

In her tennis book, *The Art of Doubles,* Pat Blaskower declares, "A winner makes commitments. A loser makes promises."[21] As in tennis, simply making promises doesn't show a long-term commitment. Reaching any goal—being a winner—requires time, effort, and sacrifice.

A Trusting Bond

Mike DeGrosky is the CEO of the Guidance Group, a consulting organization specializing in the organizational aspects of the fire service. In his article, "Teamwork Takes Trust," he explains:

> Experience in many organizations shows that successful teams focus specifically on building relationships to increase trust, and that unsuccessful teams do not... Trust deepens as members continue to experience the competency and integrity of the team and as they experience their expectations being met by other members.[22]

Great teams are confident and reliable, always backing each other when times get tough. They are never publicly critical or disrespectful toward their teammates. In committed partnerships, we learn we can be vulnerable, to trust our mate with our innermost thoughts and emotions. Confidence to be open and transparent in our relationship eliminates the need to be protective of everything we say and do when we're together.

We can only develop a climate of trust if we're always honest with each other in all aspects of what we say and do—and have no secrets from each other. With this high level of mutual trust, there ensues a natural absence of tension within the couple. Thus, a bond is created that's strong and unifying.

Team Devotion

We can, both individually and together, follow *The LoveTeam Game Plan* in setting goals that will ensure we avoid actions that pull our devotion away from our lovemate. We decide ahead of time what boundaries we need to put into place concerning our loyalties, and develop safeguards accordingly. Each person on a LoveTeam is emotionally, physically, and mentally true to their partner.

Emotionally, we should consider what books we read, what media we watch, and to whom our feelings are directed. Physically, we decide who else we hug and touch, and where we spend our time. Mentally, we ask ourselves how our thoughts are directed, how much of our time we're thinking of the other, and if our mind is committed to making our relationship stronger.

Loyal teammates anticipate what their partner's needs are and what their next move will be so they can help before being asked. Their commitment goes beyond thoughts and words—it's translated into actions.

A committed dedication to our relationship allows for trust, change, and growth. People are more motivated to change when they feel commitment from their partner. In such an atmosphere, the team will flourish. In addition, they receive assurance that the other will be with them, both in good times and bad.

As our life together begins, or when we desire something better in a more mature relationship, we make an unconditional commitment to our partner. Commitment to what? To lead a life where we do our best to be our best. And to put the team and love concepts from this book into practice for the rest of our lives. When we've knowingly decided in our mind that we're committed to our LoveTeam, we'll have a much greater chance of success.

Chapter 10
Healthy Habits are Vital

XOXO

We are what we repeatedly do.
Excellence, then, is not an act, but a habit.

~ARISTOTLE

A surgical team in a hospital works as a unit before, during, and after a surgery to ensure each patient has a positive outcome and complications are avoided. The surgeon has the major responsibility, yet works closely with, and depends on, other members of the team for the patient's well-being and constant monitoring. Other members of the surgical team usually include the anesthesiologist, the scrub nurse, and the circulating nurse. Each has his or her own duties to perform. Over time, these interrelated duties become a series of habits—a system. When each person does their respective jobs to the best of their ability, the surgery *outcome is optimal and complications are minimized.*

The interdependent duties each member of the surgical team perform don't just happen. Every member of the team has had training regarding their respective duties, practical experience with a seasoned mentor, and a certain amount of time performing the duties until they became habits. When all the regularly repeated behavioral patterns (what we call habits) are combined, a system is developed that becomes the expected, successful surgery.

In personal relationships, there are no written job descriptions as there are for a scrub nurse, for instance. There are no technical instructions as there are for driving a car, repairing a faucet, or knitting a sweater. Most couples learn through trial and error, which too often becomes crisis management. In other words, they repeat the things that are successful as they manage their daily lives. But the things that don't work become problems that need to be solved.

One way to avoid basing our relationship on crisis management is to proactively form good habits that lead to systems of doing things as a couple where the *outcome is optimal and complications are minimized*. In this way, we are prepared when something adverse happens.

Habits are the Glue

It has been said that for a habit to be established, it takes twenty-one or more consecutive repetitions. Developing these habits and systems in our relationship doesn't mean only changing ones that keep causing difficulties. It means being proactive and anticipating that a problem may eventually occur, so we build a system to prevent the trouble in the first place. This works well when both people are motivated to make their union the best it can be, when they're aware of little things that occur around them, and when they have trusting, open communication.

Sometimes there's a troublesome situation that could become a problem if not addressed. Ideally, the couple discusses it together and sets a goal to solve it. Different team approaches and possible outcomes are discussed, and the best one is decided upon. Together they develop an action plan that should lead to a consistent way of eliminating the problem. Their action plan would include which habits they will institute, with adaptations along the way when necessary.

An example of how to develop a system together is when a couple works as a team in the kitchen. One of them might cut up vegetables while the other is getting things out and beginning the cooking process. Or one might set the table while the other is preparing the beverages. By repetition, they both know what to expect each time they make a meal. They might decide to switch roles at times to have variety, but the basics of the habits ensure a predictable outcome.

Healthy habits and systems are the glue that holds a couple together. When a crisis or adversity occurs, established habits will be one aspect that moves them closer. Each partner sustains the cohesion by continuing to do the agreed-upon habits. This is one thing that will make the relationship solid, especially during difficult times.

Be Attentive—Anticipate

When you see a happy couple, what you're mainly seeing is two people who are attentive to each other and anticipate each other's needs. Their actions say, "How can I help you?" If you could go deeper into their relationship, behind closed doors so to speak, you'd see that they've made a practice of observing what their mate is or may soon be doing. We are all aware of what our needs are, but we can train our minds to concentrate on what the other may need or want. However, if giving attention to either of our individual needs could harm our LoveTeam, then it wouldn't be advisable.

How wonderful when our lovemate does the very thing we want at the precise time we need it. It's like an administrative assistant who thinks of him or herself as a team player with their supervisor. The assistant knows which file to place on their boss' desk, is conscious of their schedule for the day, and helps make life easier for them in so many ways.

We can't, of course, always predict these things with 100 percent accuracy because we can't read each other's minds. Even when we're wrong, at least our partner realizes we've tried to put ourselves in their place. In addition, there should be a habit of appreciation, like a kindly thank you, from the fortunate one who's been on the receiving end.

Deciding to be a Teammate

Certain factors contribute to the strength of bad habits: The longer a person has had them, the more extreme they are, and the more they have. It will take longer to develop good team-building habits when certain unhealthy relationship practices are well established that involve isolation, independence, or selfishness.

The decision to become a teammate is the first step toward changing bad habits. Acceptance, determination, and hard work will then propel a couple toward success. When the going gets tough, there are three kinds of people—those who just quit, those who give a half-hearted effort with many excuses, and those who go above and beyond the call of duty on a long-term quest to achieve greatness.

When one of us is struggling to overcome a bad habit so that our team is better, the other needs to be supportive and encouraging. Both partners should pull together. The struggling one may feel frustrated because they've taken two steps forward and one step back. Yet, they should realize that they're actually gaining toward the goal. If 100 is the goal, some people get to step ninety-nine and quit. Meeting the goal is sometimes just one step away, so determine to always do it one more time.

Adjusting Habits

When we're single we usually only have ourselves to consider, thus many habits are neither good nor bad. When we commit to someone else, those same habits may become a difficulty because now two people are involved. For the benefit of the team, we should both be open to adjusting certain ways of doing things to live peacefully. Habits should always be agreed upon and developed around what's best and most appropriate for each couple, but we should always be open to changing habits if they aren't working.

Have enough loving, unselfish, kind gestures and habits so that one or two of those that are forgotten or done incorrectly will be minimized and quickly forgiven. Occasional positive reinforcement is nice when one of us is trying to change a habit. However, just doing the habit to the best of one's ability should be enough for us to stay motivated as we see the positive results. Also, we don't want our relationship to become mundane, so creative adaptations can make habits fun, even though the basics of the system are still in place. Consider the adage: "Variety is the spice of life".

In athletics, proper habits that are learned early lead to a better prospect of success. The systems that are developed in sports typically don't change, whether the player is at the beginning stages or the professional ranks. For example, there's basically one best technique for holding a basketball as a player prepares to shoot. If a person is in the habit of doing it that way, they'll have more success in scoring a basket. The whole process of shooting the ball is a system that can be perfected.

The attitudes and skills that each player has will typically take them to a certain level. The correct basic techniques and systems will ultimately dictate the success they'll have in that sport. Conversely, bad practices will dramatically limit their advancement. Good sports habits are developed through repetition and hard work, as well as a commitment to practice outside the usual practice sessions. When evaluating whether to change a habit on a sports team, the details should be discussed, accepted, practiced, and possibly adapted if necessary. It's a process.

It's a comparable process for relationship habits and systems. For example, when going shopping together many couples form habits because then they know what to expect. Some of these habits may include who prepares the list of what to buy, who checks the sale ads, who drives the car, where they park, who pays the bill, and who carries the bags. The system, in this example, is the shopping trip. This process makes the trip to the mall more fun because turning these decisions into habits avoids frustration.

Everyone likes to know what to expect from their teammate, for the most part. But life isn't meant to be boring either, or so intense that we're on the edge of our seats. Systems developed from healthy habits that utilize the strengths and weaknesses of both partners minimize unmet expectations. Practicing these systems leads to a stable, loving relationship and a bond that holds a couple together during tough times.

Chapter 11
Momentum and Trends

XOXO

May you live every day of your life.
~Jonathan Swift

Team momentum determines the outcome of many athletic games, which in turn can lead to success for the season. Momentum is how a team is playing in the short run, usually for part of a game or somewhat longer. For example, if a football team is down by three touchdowns at half time, they can get momentum going in the second half by outscoring the other team, even if only in that half. It might have been a tough first half, but now the team is on a roll! In addition, this also builds momentum for future practices and the next game. Positive momentum is sometimes called "Big Mo" or "In the Zone."

A trend is the general direction of a team over a week or longer. In athletics, it's easy to see a trend in a winning season or consecutive winning seasons. Some married people talk about having the "Seven-Year Itch" or a mid-life crisis, both of which are examples of bad trends in a marital relationship. Good trends include the security by both of feeling total commitment, having a positive attitude, and becoming a LoveTeam.

Put on the Brakes

Momentum is a strength or force gained or lost by a series of events. It can be detected by a temporary shift in mood or confidence. When their team *catches fire* or goes *as cold as ice,* fans in a stadium can feel it. Similarly, a couple could have a difficult first part of the day, or possibly a tough hour. But how they come back from that will determine their momentum ending the day and going into the next day.

There are many ways to counter bad momentum. For example, if issues keep building as the day goes on, both partners would need to be more loving as soon as possible. By consciously moving physically and emotionally closer together they can change the momentum. In other words, we put forth our best effort so our relationship can *catch fire* again, and get back "In the Zone."

For a further explanation of momentum, imagine a car racing down the street. The driver of the car wants to make a right turn farther up the road. However, he doesn't see that road until just before he gets to it. Obviously he hasn't slowed down enough. The momentum keeps the car going forward, so he misses the turn! If he had applied the brakes sooner, he would have slowed his momentum enough to easily and safely make the turn.

If we want to change the direction in our relationship, like making a turn while driving, we may have to "put on the brakes." If either one senses bad momentum, they need to stop, call "Time Out," and regroup. The couple then can get the momentum going positively. A wonderful beginning to every day can be our trend when we're *a loving couple who thinks, speaks, and acts like a team.*

Upward Trend

It's important to keep our thoughts loving and team-oriented. Be perceptive when we see ourselves or our partner beginning a bad trend, such as sadness, irritation, or any mood change. Compassion may help to alter that direction. We have a choice to be positive, forgiving, cheerful, respectful, and to stick together. It's up to us to determine our direction for the day or week, and indeed for the rest of our lives. One great day can lead to another, which will then lead to an upward trend in our lives together.

Hopefully, in our relationship there are more good aspects than bad. As this positive momentum expands, it offsets the negative. With this good trend, we are then willing to let little unpleasant things go by the wayside. When we look at the big picture and determine to get on with life, we can lift each other up. A mindset of shaking off the bad keeps the momentum positive. Our partnership is more important than trivial issues.

If an aspect of their relationship seems weak, both mates should place a higher priority on improving that area. For example, if one person is impatient, he or she should admit it and make a concerted effort to be more patient. The other could act as a teammate by not only avoiding things that might cause impatience, but also being more loving. This is similar to a basketball analogy where one player shoots free throws poorly during a game. That player should practice, possibly get additional guidance, change their techniques, or whatever it takes to improve. Their teammates should encourage them.

Trends can be good, but even good trends can become boring. According to several studies, 95 percent of couples express a decline in happiness and satisfaction in the first ten years of marriage. If the reason for this decline is boredom, bringing vibrancy and a certain dynamic into the relationship can change the momentum markedly. You can plan a fun evening at a dinner theater, hike up the nearest mountain, or bring home an unexpected gift, as examples.

We should be aware of every new circumstance that enters our relationship. If it's unexpected, we'll usually just react without thinking. But afterward we should discuss how we will handle this circumstance if it's likely to be repeated, to avoid irritation or conflict. Two examples are the following: If one person gets a new job that requires a longer commute, the couple should discuss how they will rework the changes this will mean in their lives, like the extra time, cost of gasoline, or additional stress. Another example is when someone calls at 10 p.m. and we've agreed that the evening after 9 p.m. is our private time. Do we just not answer the phone, or take the call but tactfully tell the person calling we don't like to be called after 9 p.m?

Changing a trend is about opposites: Is life going too fast? Then spend some quiet time together. Do you sense a lack of affection? Then be extra loving. It's all about bringing balance into our relationship. The most important trend that may need to be balanced by many couples is the trend to form a team. Since you're just learning these concepts, it will take a concerted effort to change non-team trends. These include turning downward trends like living isolated lives and being negative, into upward trends like developing a "we" mentality and giving encouragement. It's exciting that becoming a LoveTeam can be a new trend for you!

Progress

One of the key elements of success on any team is that there's progress. Hopefully the progress is consistent and the trend is going toward improvement in our relationship. However, it may be ten steps forward and nine steps backward. That isn't stagnation nor digression—it's forward movement.

On a sports team, when the players know they're successful they feel closer to each other. Similarly, when we know we're successful, most days end by feeling closer to our lovemate. We may have turned a bad day into good, or turned a good day into one that is great. Thus, we can wake up most mornings feeling awesome.

As you look at your relationship over the next year, feeling closer and being happier should be the trend. If you're making progress every day or every week, even to a small degree, years from now you'll be markedly improved—a gradual upward angle. Be aware of this and celebrate it!

In a mature partnership, it may take several months to forgive events of the past, get on the right track, and go forward toward your *LoveTeam Game Plan* goals. But no matter where you are in your relationship, now is always a good time to positively change your momentum. You can be "In the Zone" sooner than you think.

xoxo
Team Completion

Chapter 12
Unify Our Needs

XOXO

*I am a member of a team, and I rely on the team,
I defer to it and sacrifice for it, because the team,
not the individual, is the ultimate champion.*

~Mia Hamm

Why do people marry or enter into committed relationships? One reason is that we assume our partner will meet most of our needs and our expectations. In other words, we think that we'll be fulfilled in a way we weren't when we were single. The reality is that by being on a LoveTeam a person can get most of their needs met by a supportive mate. Even better, though, is the opportunity to be the person who gives that support, which can be even more satisfying. To have a great relationship, however, what each individual wants or needs should be evaluated by whether it helps or harms their particular team.

It's a concept that's present in all other successful teams as well. In business, for instance, good companies meet many individual employees' needs in order to succeed in their business ventures as long as what the employees want is good for the company. Successful companies will work with individuals to make the workplace an employee-friendly environment, but their main purpose is to ensure that the goals of the company are met.

Individual Needs Versus Team Needs

On self-managed teams, including couple teams, one member directly affects their teammate when they're concentrating more on what they individually want rather than if it's good for the team. For example, on a two-person beach volleyball team, the team's expectations were discussed and agreed upon by both players before the games began. They decided together that success would mean winning at least two of their matches that day. Yet during the games, one player wanted newspaper publicity so she recklessly spiked the ball, frequently hitting the net or going out of bounds. Although she made some flashy moves to get her name and picture in the paper, the team lost all their games. Therefore, the team's expectations for that day weren't met.

Another example of how one teammate affects the other is when a couple marries and it becomes obvious that the sleeping patterns for each of them are quite different. The wife has always had eight hours of sleep, but the husband has previously slept only six hours. First, they both try sleeping for seven hours, but the wife is tired and feels poorly the next day. Then they try a plan where the wife sleeps for eight hours, and the husband gets up after six and reads the newspaper. This doesn't work either because one of their goals is to start the day together. Finally, they decide they'll both sleep for close to eight hours. In time, the husband adjusts to sleeping longer, they get up together in the morning, and their goal is met. An unforeseen benefit is that the husband feels better than he has in a long time. There can usually be a win/win result if we work together to find the best solution.

Ideally, our major individual needs and goals should be discussed before we enter into a committed relationship. However if we already are in such a relationship, we should talk about any unexpressed desires at our next opportunity. Otherwise, unfulfilled needs can become frustrations that won't help our LoveTeam. When discussing these needs, focus on how our decisions will affect us as a unit. (See Chapter 25, "Communication")

The Process

Here is a process that works for avoiding frustrations when our desires aren't met. There are five steps to unifying our individual needs with our team's needs. They are:

- ✦ It is first necessary for each of us to lovingly verbalize our individual needs and expectations, keeping our team in mind. So many people feel their needs aren't being met but they may never have expressed them fully. And many people assume their mate wants the same things they do, but this may not be the case.
- ✦ Become familiar with and understand what our teammate wants and expects. It's important that everything is very clear and, if necessary, ask for clarification and examples.
- ✦ Next, discuss what's best for our team, remembering to be realistic and flexible. Before deciding, the plan should be evaluated to make sure it will move the couple closer together, and be healthy—emotionally, mentally, physically and, for some, spiritually. This may take several discussions to ponder the situation before coming to a definite conclusion, remembering to think outside the box.

- Determine that we'll work together to form habits that will meet our new goals. We then put what is decided into practice, giving our best effort to succeed.
- Occasionally evaluate how the plan is working. If it isn't, more discussion may be needed—go back to the drawing board, so to speak, and go through the process again to make any necessary adjustments.

It's helpful for us to spend as much time as necessary discussing relevant issues, even if they seem unimportant to one of us. In addition, we should realize that we might not be able to have everything exactly the way we individually want. As a team, there are now two people to be considered. But it's also true that some of the needs we had as a single person weren't met by being single, or we wouldn't have wanted to become committed to our relationship. This is what is so satisfying about having a partner—so much of what we want in life can only be met by being part of a two-person team.

Some More Examples

Let's consider an ice skating pair. Before they became partners, it was important for them to determine that their professional goals were similar. They discovered that both of them wanted to win an Olympic gold medal. When they agreed on this major goal, they decided to become partners.

Next they discussed how to get to that goal. Concerning practice sessions, one partner thought she needed six hours of training a day, while the other felt he needed ten, but they had to practice together. They decided that a compromise of eight hours would probably not be the best answer since one partner knew from experience it wasn't enough practice time for him with such a lofty goal. So first they decided to practice ten hours a day. Yet, she was getting too tired, so they agreed to cut the time down to nine hours and take fewer breaks. In other words, they were open to reevaluating and making adjustments to meet their team's needs.

In another example, a husband liked to socialize, yet his wife didn't enjoy having people over to their home. His wife liked to go to the theater more than he did. They realized that these issues could become a problem if they didn't solve them, so they discussed the expectations each of them had. It was initially decided that they would invite a couple to meet them at the theater, then go to a restaurant together and talk over dessert. They tried this plan, but after the first night they both were so tired after the theater that neither of them enjoyed the dessert date. What worked for them was to meet another couple at a restaurant several evenings a month. And another evening they'd go to the theater by themselves. Consequently, they both looked forward to their nights out. This example shows that it may take time, but everything can be worked out when both think as a team.

Some of each individual's needs will be acceptable to adopt as team goals. For example, a wife may have a desire to play the piano. Her husband agrees to support her and to watch their children while she practices. So, she enjoys practicing the piano daily to meet one of her needs and her husband discovers spending that time with the children is fun. An added bonus: they all learn to appreciate music.

Accountability

In our most important relationship, accountability gives us an unusual advantage. It's unusual because many people wouldn't see it as an advantage, but when one thinks deeply about it, it truly is a positive. We have a trusted person who will hold us accountable when we ask. To be accountable means the obligation to report, explain, or justify something, to be responsible or answerable. How is this good?

Say you want to stop biting your fingernails. It's a known fact that it's easier to break a habit when you've shared your plan with someone else. This way you have a supportive person who can cheer you on when you do well, and give you a pep talk when you mess up. However, this accountability concept only works well when the person with the bad habit asks to be held accountable.

Our lovemate should be the only person whom we ask to hold us accountable for habits and actions involving our relationship. If we ask other people to hold us accountable for these situations, we will be diminishing the trust in our partnership. Also, they may give advice contrary to our team goals. They have no right to know private details of our relationship and may even side with either one, which could harm our team.

There are other aspects of accountability that make it an advantage. Being held accountable is good because it helps us to grow. As we are changing, our mate isn't critical but helpful because they're doing what we've requested. We should remember that they aren't responsible for our behavior, but are involved to give support, encouragement, and keep us on track.

From the article, "Accountability in Your Marriage," on the website feedtherightwolf.org, Kay Jones writes:

> Accountability isn't just a concern for recovering addicts. It is crucial in any relationship, and it applies to both partners. If either partner is acting in a way that is unhealthy for him or her, contrary to his or her stated goals or principles, or isn't in the best interests of the relationship, it is the other partner's responsibility to hold him or her accountable for that behavior.

It is important to remember that it is not your job to punish or judge your spouse, or to force him or her to stop or change the unhealthy behavior. You are *never* responsible for your partner's actions or decisions. Your role as a spouse is simply to point out, firmly but lovingly, that your partner is getting off track. What he or she does with that information is out of your hands.[23]

We're fortunate to have and be an accountability partner. It can be a big part of adjusting habits that will make each of us the best person we can be, and the best team we can be!

In summary, our individual desires are always secondary to what's best for our relationship as a whole. However, when our LoveTeam is functioning well, the needs that are important to each individual are considered and generally met, possibly in unexpected ways. When lovingly discussed and decided together, a couple's new plans usually turn out better for both partners, they have the advantage of an accountability partner, and this results in a win/win for both.

Chapter 13
Enjoy Our Differences

XOXO

Teamwork divides the task and doubles the success.
~A<small>NONYMOUS</small>

A person looks at a flying bird and is fascinated by the uncomplicated beauty of it. Conversely, a bird expert observes the same bird in flight and notices the lay of the feathers, their wingspan, or other intricate details. He might not appreciate the simple beauty. Neither is wrong in how they see the bird, but together, after discussing what they saw, they'd be able to acknowledge the benefits of enjoying the bird from both perspectives.

In the areas of business, athletics, or relationships, each member of a team doesn't have to know everything or have all the abilities necessary to contribute to the team success. What is significant is that at least one member of the team has the know-how in important areas, or they can get expert advice outside the team. On a basketball team, every player doesn't have to be a good rebounder, shooter, and dribbler; at least one player, though, needs to be proficient in each skill for the team to be great.

In a company that makes deep-sea equipment, for instance, engineers design the products, factory workers produce and assemble them, and warehouse personnel ship them out to the customers. For the company to meet their goals, each department must function as an effective team, and all departments must coordinate their efforts together.

Similarly, in personal relationships it's desirable that each person brings different strengths to their LoveTeam. People understand that on athletic teams there needs to be a balance of talents to be successful. Or in manufacturing companies there are reasons for employees to have different functions and skills. It's also true that differences are what make a relationship the best it can be.

Debunking the Myth

Some individuals have come to believe that gender differences are a major and somewhat negative factor in relationships. In the book *Just Your Type*, the authors "debunk the myth that it's all about gender." As they explain:

> A whole industry has been created around the notion that gender is to blame: men and women are so inherently different that they don't even come from the same planet! Since they don't, won't, and can't speak the same language, they can never be expected to understand each other, much less communicate well.
>
> Most people would agree that men and women *are* different, and in some very profound ways. Some women do fit the female stereotype of being sensitive, emotional, nurturing, and open, just as some men

fit the male stereotype of being tough, competitive, emotionally self-contained, and independent. But as our research study demonstrated, it turns out these men and women represent only between thirty and forty percent of the American population.[24]

Obviously gender is one factor in our being different from our mate, but we believe that this difference is a completing of each other. It's a blending of the male and female characteristics to the advantage of our union. However, it's also our inherent personalities, characteristics, backgrounds, environment, and experiences which make us individually who we are, whether male or female.

We're All Different

Fortunately, no two people are clones of each other. It's ironic that people, when looking for a lifelong mate, think the best choice would be someone who's very similar to them. In fact, they may spend years trying to find someone who's the most like them. Yet, they would do well to imagine these scenarios:

- Both partners are talkative, so they often verbally compete with each other when together and in social situations.
- Neither has had experience playing or watching sports, so they never attend, play, or watch anything involving athletics, thus making it difficult to relate to anyone who does.
- Both are creative and innovative, but have a difficult time finishing projects because they lose motivation.
- They spend the majority of their leisure time cleaning because both are meticulous about keeping the house clean.

- Neither likes to cook, so they eat out nearly every night, becoming unhealthy and draining their budget.
- Husband and wife own a small business and both are detail-oriented, so they have difficulty grasping the big-picture concepts necessary to succeed.

It's not a bad thing when a couple has similar characteristics, as in the above scenarios. But it's also not a bad thing when they have differences—they can have a broader view of the world.

Another example of how a similar characteristic doesn't help the team is when neither has the desire or skills to complete their taxes. They discuss together their options. They could hire someone to do them, they could do their own taxes after taking a course, or they could just not do their taxes. (We didn't say they were all good solutions!) If one was more adept with taxes, it would benefit the partnership and thus complete their team.

Similar and Different

All couples have similarities and differences—what advantages they have! If one partner always plans ahead and the other is spontaneous, a balance is created. Likewise, it can be useful if one is good with math and the other has an interest in music. And if one has the strength to do heavy chores and the other takes on the projects that require a soft touch, their team can be made complete in that area.

We know a man who had dated a woman who was quiet, like he was. He realized he had a personality trait that could be improved with the right person by his side. So he then began dating another woman who was more talkative and socially adept. She brought him into conversations with others. Guess what—he married her!

Couples think they will be the happiest if they are similar to each other. It's true they may initially have fewer issues to resolve, but they may not become as complete nor have as much variety in their lives. If they choose someone who is very different from them, they may have to work through more issues early on. However, they will soon appreciate how the other completes them and their lives will have more diversity—and excitement. Whether they're similar to each other or very different, they can, indeed, have a very fulfilling life.

Referring again to the book *Just Your Type*, the authors initially ask the couples reading the book to identify their individual personality type from sixteen non-gender options. Next, they explain the joys of their combined types, followed by the possible frustrations that could be present with pairing these two personalities. Lastly, they tell the best way to relate to and appreciate their partner who is different from them.[25] It's helpful to know why our lovemate thinks the way they do—understanding goes a long way in becoming a team.

Harmony and Completion

In choral groups, when one person sings, it sounds a certain way. When two or more people sing in harmony—different notes for each person—they blend together to the delight of the audience. Just as this orchestrating of sounds is important in making beautiful music, harmonizing our personalities does a lot to encourage unity and vitality.

As you dated, you came to recognize that this person would be a great match for you. As examples, maybe you found early on that you both liked the same type of restaurants, activities, sports, or music. Yet, you also realized that their storytelling ability, which you lacked, would make your life more enjoyable. Or, that your expertise in gourmet cooking would complement their less diverse eating habits. Another possibility—your reserve in showing affection could be nicely developed by this abundantly loving person.

Usually most dating couples can relate to some of the preceding examples, realizing they're alike in some areas and different in others. As time goes on, hopefully the differences they enjoyed previously stay as pluses, and they expand the things complementary about each other.

We have more potential to be complete when both of us are open to making changes in our views and actions. After all, our way isn't the only way. We may have to go outside our comfort zone for the good of our team, which is more important than either of us as two individuals.

Someone once said, "A committed team can overcome obstacles by pulling together and combining their individual strengths." Respecting and enjoying each other's differences bring so many benefits. We have the opportunity to learn from each other, see things from a different perspective, and grow in exciting ways that weren't possible before becoming a LoveTeam.

Chapter 14

Making Changes and Adjustments

XOXO

> *By changing nothing, nothing changes.*
> ~Tony Robbins

It's rare when an individual comes into a relationship expecting to make personal changes. Even if they do anticipate making some adjustments, normally they don't expect to change very much. Usually they want to stay comfortable with the way they did things when they led a single life or the way their family did things. Additionally, each may expect just the opposite of their new relationship: One may want to settle in with the same comfortable routines they previously knew and liked, while the other may want life to be completely different from their prior life. If they're divorced or widowed, a person may expect this new relationship to be the same or completely different, depending on the level of contentment they had previously.

When people are dating, they obviously don't know what their relationship will ultimately become in the long run. But they may have some preconceived hopes. In order to be successful, both people need to develop a team attitude of being open-minded about making the necessary changes that will benefit their developing relationship. In fact, being eager to make changes is important because they realize that the advantages of making helpful adjustments will far outweigh the disadvantages of not making them.

Changes are Inevitable

Whenever we join any team, we should expect to make some changes. In sports, if a baseball player has previously been a catcher but the team he joins only needs a third baseman, he'll have to switch positions. The skills for a third baseman are different from those of a catcher. For instance, on a ground ball a catcher may drop to the ground to block a ball in the dirt, whereas a third baseman doesn't have the time to drop to the ground and still throw the runner out at first base.

The baseball player may have to change not just his position but also his role on the team. One major responsibility of a catcher is encouraging and guiding a pitcher during the game by walking out to the mound to confer with him. As a third baseman, his new role with the pitcher is to shout encouragement from his position. To be a contributing member of that team, he needs to accept the change and strive to be the best third baseman possible.

What are occurrences that usually cause changes, good or bad, in a relationship? Some of the most common reasons are a crisis (such as a bankruptcy), a traumatic event (a house fire), or a life-changing situation (the birth of a baby). None of these scenarios should hamper them. On the contrary, a LoveTeam is designed so that these types of stresses would bring a couple closer. This would naturally happen because we have a lovemate: A person who feels that the other is always on our side, loves us, has empathy, and a desire to help and make sacrifices. This doesn't usually happen without some work on the couple's part prior to the occurrence. When a couple has proactively built their team into a close and loving partnership, adversity and life-changing situations only draw them together.

Too many mates aren't willing to make changes and don't see the value in doing so. Why is this the case? Mainly because everywhere they look they're bombarded with the attitude that their individuality is more important than their relationship. Sadly, in our current society individuals are often highlighted much more than happy couples. What they almost never hear are the huge advantages of being on a LoveTeam.

Couples might be motivated to change for several reasons: When someone models desirable behavior for them, or when they see the positive results of little improvements they make. But the best motivations for positive change are becoming aware of the helpful team concepts and learning how important love is in their relationship. In other words, they adopt and practice the goal introduced in Part One: to become a LoveTeam, and follow *The LoveTeam Game Plan: for a loving couple to think, speak, and act like a team.*

Flexibility

There must be a starting point for any changes made, and flexibility is a big part of that. On a corporate team, one of the employees is scheduled to do an important presentation to a client. That employee finds out he has to have surgery before the presentation, so isn't going to be available. One of the other team members agrees to do the presentation, even though public speaking is very uncomfortable for her. Before the scheduled presentation, she takes a quick course in public speaking, and becomes familiar with the presentation material so that she's prepared. She does her best the day of the presentation.

Soon afterward, because her supervisors value team-oriented employees, she is promoted.

A great relationship happens more readily if both partners decide to become the best they can be for their team. Either one should happily make a lifestyle change or moderate a personality trait when they agree it would be an improvement. Accepting a healthier diet, spending more time together, and only speaking positively about each other are some examples. An individual's level of being flexible, their willingness to make changes, and a desire to do their best results in a stronger and more trusting team.

Consider the story, *The Burmese Monkey Trap:*

> In southern Myanmar, some hill tribes still hunt monkeys for food. Monkeys are rather intelligent, and yet they are caught with a very simple trap. The hunters drill a hole in a coconut just large enough for a monkey to get a paw in. They fill the coconut with peanuts and tie it to a tree with wire. When a monkey smells the peanuts, he approaches the coconut. The monkey plays with the coconut, but the shape of the hole (a cone) makes it very difficult to get the peanuts out. So the eager monkey pushes its tiny paw in and manages to grab some of the peanuts. The monkey then tries to flee with his loot, but the coconut is tied to the tree. His paw filled with peanuts is too big to pull out of the coconut, and so he is trapped. In the morning, the hunter approaches. The monkey is terrified but cannot release itself from the trap. He cannot let go.[26]

As with the monkey in the story, sometimes our desire to hold onto habits that aren't constructive for our relationship is greater than our desire to change. If so, we will be like the monkey, *caught* in not being able to meet our goal of becoming a LoveTeam. Unfortunately, this will negatively impact our partner as well.

Always Evolving

What's our perspective in making changes? Let's say a person has overused her shoulder to the point that it now has a very limited range of motion, commonly called frozen shoulder. Her physical therapist tells her she has three options:

- Do nothing and live the rest of her life with the limitation.
- Have her shoulder surgically repaired, or manipulated, under anesthesia. The surgery, a quick fix, isn't always successful and there are risks involved. She would still need physical therapy afterward to maintain the motion that was achieved during surgery.
- Practice daily exercises at home that are painful. This usually takes several months to accomplish the slow release of the frozen shoulder, but there are very few risks.

As in the last option above, are you willing to spend time every day and give the necessary effort to have the best partnership you can? The alternative is to accept things as they are. There is no quick fix as in the second option above.

Making positive changes in a relationship may take months to implement. Patience and support are necessary from each lovemate as adjustments are made. It takes a willing attitude, and an awareness that there may be several steps for some changes. If making these modifications will help our team, even if it does take months, it will be worth the effort in the long run.

A boy was swimming in shallow water at the beach. After awhile, he looked up and noticed that his parents were way down the beach. He had drifted down the coast and didn't realize it. The movement from his original location wasn't noticeable, but the results were significant. In a similar way, small changes in a relationship may be subtle and not easily noticed, but over months or years, positive adjustments can make a significant impact. Just the fact that we're willing to change for our LoveTeam goes a long way in showing our partner how important they are in our lives.

Improvements are not always easy and ongoing communication is required. Whether in sports, business, or relationships, it's important for a team to continue evolving, and to decide together what changes will be the most beneficial. Later, minor adjustments to decisions can be made as things come up, as they inevitably will in life. As Winston Churchill said, "Success is the ability to go from one failure to another with no loss of enthusiasm."

Some people may ask, "Do I have to lose some of myself to have a successful relationship?" Consider this example: You usually get up at 10 a.m., but your new job requires you to be there by 8 a.m. Was it a bad thing that you used to sleep until 10 a.m? No, but you still have to change the time you get up if you want to keep that job. Is there an incentive to getting up earlier? Yes—you get a paycheck! Similarly, the changes you make for your LoveTeam will pay great dividends.

In other areas of our lives, we are willing to change—even overnight. For example, in our workplace we may need to accept a new dress code, go paperless, or be assigned different responsibilities. Since our relationship is more significant to us than a job, how quickly we respond to changes that will help us is more critical.

Success Requires Change

A LoveTeam responds to the changing needs of each other and also to outside influences. Risk-taking and creativity are encouraged, and mistakes are treated as sources of learning. These are all part of the process of team improvement. As changes are made, support and patience are valued.

Some lines are pertinent from the movie *Miracle,* about the gold medal winning 1980 Olympic hockey team, to show the importance of change in becoming successful. This is what Herb Brooks said in the movie to the US Olympic Committee when he was being interviewed for the job of coach:

> The only way we can compete with the Eastern Bloc teams is if we're willing to change. Change the way we train, the way we prepare, even change our schedule. We also need to change the way we play the game.[27]

In another movie *Hoosiers,* a parent volunteer coach said that the high school basketball team always played zone defense. He urged the new coach not to mess up the boys by teaching a man-to-man defense, since the team had made it to the state semifinals the previous year. However, the new coach changed the defense to man-to-man, adjusted the boys' attitudes, and altered their entire style of play. The result—this small town team won the state championship![28]

This chapter isn't meant to give a person the expectation that their partner should do any or all of the changing. In fact, the only person we can change is ourselves. However, if we'd like our teammate to adjust something they do and we think the timing is right, we can talk to them lovingly and without confrontation. Hopefully they will understand and make the commitment to change. But, if not, we happily accept their decision because the timing may not be right, or it might be us who needs to adjust our thinking to benefit the team. In any case, we continue to be loving and patient. If we do, there's a much better chance that positive changes will occur.

Since we're a self-managed team, we don't have someone else telling us what adaptations to make to improve our team. The two of us are empowered on our own to communicate well, admit when we need to make changes, and put those changes into practice. As a result, our twosome will be stronger and we'll feel like we're winning a state championship every day!

Chapter 15
Balance

XOXO

Next to love, balance is the most important thing.
~John Wooden

It's always interesting to observe a happy couple after decades of marriage. If we could find out what each of them was like before they married and compare that to what each of them is like now, it might surprise some people. There are couples who stay together simply because they think no one else would want them! We believe, however, that most couples who are truly joyful applied many of the LoveTeam concepts without even knowing it as they grew closer through the years. They learned from the past and moved forward in their relationship.

Most likely what happy couples have found in their lives together is balance. Balance led them to not take each other for granted, to appropriately prioritize, and to form comfortable, dependable, loving habits. Did they have to give up some of what each of them used to be? Surely they did. If you ask these partners if it was worth it, each would most likely say "yes" without a pause. They unknowingly developed *The LoveTeam Game Plan* concepts into their relationship and became a loving team.

Mental Balance

It's so important to keep a positive perspective, to look at the so-called half-full cup in our partnership. Do we balance the successes with the failures, the things to appreciate with those to be minimized? It's especially important to keep the right mental balance during times of crisis and adversity, as athletes do when they "come through in the clutch."

Balance in a relationship is not just give and take, or even compromise in the traditional sense of meeting halfway. It involves coming up with the best option for the two of us as a team, which usually involves thinking creatively together. In addition, there may be several habits of our partner that we decide to overlook for the betterment of our team. Our mate is so awesome in most everything else, we choose to accept the total person.

Are we balanced in our thoughts? Are we thinking mostly about work when we're home? Are we thinking about our hobbies, relatives, or problems when we're on a date together? Our thoughts guide us and reveal what really is important to us. They can be redirected appropriately, though, if we have the desire, a proactive action plan and are willing to give our best effort.

Balance in Time and Energy

How much time do we spend in each of our activities, and are these time segments proportional to our top priorities? The same questions can be asked regarding our energy and our patience. Do our actions reflect what's most important? We may have to do some soul searching to determine if changes should be made to balance out these priorities.

When we look at our relationship, our perspective should be based on the long-term, not a particular hour, day or even week, because most things adjust with time. For example, in the first few weeks and months after the arrival of a baby, the family changes are dramatic. The baby is small and needs a lot of attention and care. However, it's important for the new parents to know that it won't always be that way. The infant will grow and need less attention as time goes on.

Obviously, a great deal of our time will be spent in earning a living and doing mundane chores—things that we don't necessarily like to do but that need to be done nonetheless. When we choose a career, determine hobbies, and decide what our lifestyle will be, do we carefully consider if these allow enough time with our loved ones? Balancing the household responsibilities with our partner will increase our efficiency, our flexibility, and our time together, thus resulting in a more harmonious, team-oriented relationship.

It would be an interesting exercise to envision the final days of our lives and evaluate what our thoughts might be at that time. Would we say to ourselves, "I wish I had spent more hours at work, at my hobby, playing sports, or with friends"? Or would we say, "I wish I had given more time and energy to my relationship and family"? *If only* may be the saddest phrase in the English language because we all want to live with no regrets. It's never too late to evaluate our lives and make changes regarding what we value most. Will that include becoming a LoveTeam?

Emotional Balance

In any one day, we have only so much emotional energy to give before it starts to take its toll. It can be depleted as easily as our physical energy. It's important to know that we can control how much of our emotions we give in a day and where it's directed.

We may have to put limits or stops on certain activities, relationships, or situations to ensure that our partnership is protected.

In doubles tennis, the following quote explains how emotional balance can complete a team. From *The Art of Doubles:*

> Once you've canvassed the field and have your eye on a few winners [teammates], look for someone in this group who complements you emotionally. If you tend to rush through matches, sometimes even holding your breath during points, don't pick someone who is in as mad a rush as you are. Your play will look like a fast-forward image. You will never gain balance as a team and will probably wear each other out before the first set is over. Choose someone whose internal clock runs a little more slowly than yours and who can get you to pause and take an occasional deep breath. Conversely, if you are a plodder who prefers to think slowly and carefully, pick someone who can rev your motor a little and help you turn up the tempo of a match.
>
> Emotional balance may not seem so vital, but is critical to the rhythm of your teamwork. During a match, the time you spend not hitting a ball—the between-points time—far exceeds the time you actually spend playing a point. What a team does during the between-points time will often determine whether it can maintain momentum within a match, and whether it can steal momentum from the opposition while they are napping. In addition, the team that manages this down time better, using it to change strategy, suggest a play, or give added encouragement to one another, will almost always be the victor in a tight match.[29]

Many couples have a difficult time finding the right emotional balance. They might see the "Big Picture" better when they can appreciate all the positive aspects of their relationship, and the negatives will easily be offset by all the good. We, personally, make scrapbooks out of our photographs, ticket stubs, brochures, and memorabilia that we collect when we do things together. As we look through the scrapbooks, we celebrate the good times and the fun experiences, appreciating how we've grown together through the years. You might try similar traditions that can keep you close when your relationship is great, and that can bring you together when you need a boost.

When our mate has a reasonable request, it's almost always best to honor it. We may think that what our partner is requesting is no big deal, but it *is* a big deal if it affects them, and thus our team. Balance how we may think about something with how the other is telling us they think. There are no little things in a relationship; if something bothers one person, solve it before it becomes a problem.

There is one area, however, where balance has no place in relationships—moral issues. A person is either honest or they aren't; they keep confidences or they don't; they have courage respecting ethical issues or not; they're sexually moral or they're not. The scale always tips all the way to one side where morality is concerned.

The Right Balance

There are basketball teams that are strong in offense but weak in defense. They practice fundamentals like shooting and passing, but seldom practice defensive skills like guarding or stance. This team would have very little success against a team that is strong in both areas.

Another example is in the human body. Two of the major organs are the heart and brain. For the body to function, the heart has to have signals from the brain to give it the power to pump. Within the heart and brain are also other processes that have to be working correctly for the whole system to work. If any of these processes aren't optimal, the person would have health problems.

A third example is with a car. To drive a car, the motor and transmission both need to be in working order. When you put the car into drive, if either of these two major components is malfunctioning, the car won't move. Since both the motor and transmission have more than one part, many intricate elements of each have to be working correctly.

We have given the three preceding examples to illustrate the importance and the basic simplicity of having the two essential parts in your relationship to make it great: Love and Team. Like the basketball team's offense and defense, the body's heart and brain, and the car's motor and transmission, all elements need to be functioning at their highest levels. If they aren't, there won't be a winning basketball team, a strong body, a dependable car, or a great LoveTeam.

In addition, the major components of the above examples are multifaceted. For instance, the car's motor compartment is made up of many parts, like a starter and a battery. In a like way, each of the two relationship parts of love and team are made up of many factors. The previous chapters of Part Two: "The Power of Team," have already discussed the team elements. It's important for all of these subjects to be integrated into our union.

Equally important are the following chapters in Part Three: "The Power of Love." It's just as vital for all of the following topics in the upcoming chapters to be put into practice for our relationship to function optimally, like in the above examples of the basketball team, the body, and the car. A couple needs to equalize the team aspects with the love aspects to reach their goal of becoming a "Snapshots" couple.

Certainly it will take time, effort, and determination by both of you, so it won't happen overnight. We hope you will commit to putting these ideas into your daily lives in your own way. These are the fundamentals that are lacking in most relationships today, and the main reason why so many are failing.

Next you will be learning about topics that will enliven the love you have, such as affection, fun, excitement, and becoming best friends. Bringing these wonderful aspects of love into your relationship will change your direction so you can now achieve the right balance—and become a LoveTeam.

Part Three

The Power of Love

XOXO

A successful team beats with one heart.
~Anonymous

In review, the success of a sports, business, or personal relationship team depends on developing three aspects of becoming a team as previously discussed—spirit, fundamentals, and completion. When team members have developed competence leading to excellence in all of these, they have a much improved chance of succeeding.

Picture a sports or business team where a player or employee wants all the glory for himself. Or he is critical of his teammates, doesn't follow the game plan, or won't make necessary changes. Success for this team would be diminished proportionately by two factors: how many players or employees don't utilize team elements, and the number of team aspects that aren't applied.

Fortunately, couples reading this book now realize that most of the factors that ensure success in athletics or business also play a major role in ensuring success in their relationship. Applying these team concepts is crucial to becoming a "Snapshots" couple. However, athletic teams, business teams, and most other teams lack one essential feature that must also be present to make a relationship great—*love*. LOVE is equally as important as TEAM to have balance as a couple. The remainder of this book will be devoted to helping you understand the love aspects and the part they play on your LoveTeam.

A Blend of Two

Planting a corn seed is like the blending of team with love. The seed is planted at the right depth in fertile soil with favorable conditions. Even though it has plenty of sunshine, it doesn't rain after the seedling emerges. Without water, the seedling withers and dies. Similarly, if it rains just the right amount, but the seed was planted where it doesn't get any sunshine, it would die then, too. When the seedling gets the right amounts of water *and* light, it becomes a healthy and productive corn stalk.

Relationships usually start out similar to the seedling. Most couples begin with abundant love. Yet, if the twelve factors of team aren't practiced, their partnership won't continue to thrive as it could. It's also true that even if the couple has cultivated the team ideas but love isn't strong in their relationship, their union won't grow and blossom.

There's a type of industrial adhesive called "epoxy" that comes packaged with two separate chemicals. It requires combining the two for the epoxy to do its work. Each is a catalyst for the other. When combined, the epoxy has industrial-strength binding qualities. These types of adhesives are used in making automobiles, aircraft, bicycles, boats, golf clubs, skis, snowboards and the like. Can you imagine the disastrous consequences for consumers if these two chemicals don't bond well?

Love and team are like these two adhesive chemicals. One without the other won't be adequate, and they must be in the correct proportions. Together these two factors are needed equally and in abundance for a relationship to bond and grow to its maximum capability. Without this binding power, disaster could be the result.

A Filtering System

A word of warning to couples: People come from many complicated backgrounds. When they become committed, it goes without saying that many aspects of their previous lives will automatically be carried over into their relationship. To become a LoveTeam, there's no doubt that each one will have to leave their single and family comfort zones. They'll need to accept, embrace, and develop their new comfort zones as two equal partners.

Couples should have a "filtering system" to help them get rid of past unacceptable habits, practices, and beliefs. The relationship will be affected sooner or later by these carryovers, and can be destructive to the evolving relationship. The couple may also need to use a filtering system to weed out outside influences that have a negative impact. These include activities, interests, media, or people. If they don't filter these out, the couple might be in for a *long* fifty years.

Certain ways of doing things or habits that may also need to be filtered out are obvious because they're almost always destructive to a relationship. Others are more subtle and may be acceptable to keep with a few modifications agreed upon by the couple. Examples won't be given here because we believe couples should make their own decisions as to what is desirable to filter out so they can have a loving, team-like partnership custom fit to them. Thus, they become empowered to cooperatively develop solutions.

However, it isn't just those things that are brought into the new committed relationship that are a concern. There are habits, interests, influences, and ways of doing things that might enter in after a relationship is established. These should also be filtered as soon as they appear. Being proactive is preferable to having to put a halt to something that's already in place. Without proactively employing this filtering system, love can fade. It's vital to protect our relationship from destructive influences that come from outside our relationship or from either one of us.

A Great Need

One of the greatest, if not the greatest, need all human beings have is to be loved and know someone cares about them. We need to feel love from our parents, siblings, and others when we are young. When we grow up, the search begins for one special person to love and be loved by. Some people learn loving actions and words from their parents and find it easy to give love to their mate. Others may not be as comfortable being loving and affectionate. It is, however, something that can be learned.

Love is a deep, tender feeling of affection and caring concern for the well-being of another. Especially with our mate we want a loving attitude that leads to loving actions. So, as a way to keep our adoration growing, we can expand on the earliest feelings of love we had for each other.

How beautiful to wake up every day with thoughts of affection and care for our lovemate. These uplifting emotions should be foremost in our minds every day. Otherwise, it becomes easier for something else to dominate our thoughts, possibly even considerations that are destructive to our relationship. Obviously this would not be good for our team, our priority.

Since opposite emotions of love are hostility or apathy, think how cancerous these are when two people are attempting to have a close partnership. The best way to overcome hostility and apathy is to replace them with loving thoughts and actions.

Always remember, a great relationship is a LoveTeam: *a loving couple who thinks, speaks, and acts like a team.*

In the remainder of Part Three, many important love aspects will be considered. Some people might not be aware that *abundant* love is essential throughout a long term relationship. Yet we know it's so important that it warrants half of this book. The upcoming chapters will include appreciation and respect for our mate, how much fun it is to be with our best friend, and the importance of loving communication.

Since love is such a beautiful and powerful aspect of a relationship, couples should do everything they can to encourage their love to grow and blossom. Let's discover how LOVE blended with TEAM can ensure a joyful, abundant life together.

XOXO
Our Lives Together

Chapter 16

Best Friends

XOXO

If I can stop one heart from breaking, I shall not live in vain.
~Emily Dickinson

There was a commercial on television several years ago: A middle-aged couple is standing outside their home watching their last child go off to college. As she drives away, they look at each other and smile broadly. In the next scene, they're having a blast together at an amusement park, screaming and laughing on a roller coaster!

This couple realized that in spite of becoming empty nesters, they still had each other. Their world didn't fall down around them when they were alone in their home without the children. On the contrary, they now had more time to devote to each other—a new era of love, playfulness, and excitement. How did they get to this point?

Closest Confidant

This empty-nest couple appeared to think that their spouse was their one-of-a-kind best friend and closest confidant. A best-selling author of books on couple relationships, Harville Hendrix said, "Marriage, ultimately, is the practice of becoming passionate friends."

Unfortunately, many people refer to a friend of the same sex, a relative, or even to their dog as their "best friend." What message is this sending to their mate? The word *best* means of the highest standing or the most important. We may have good friends, but we can only have one best friend.

For most of us, our dating relationship began as a friendship. It then grew into love as the qualities that are important in a friendship expanded and deepened. After that, affection and romance were added. As time goes on, it's important that the friendship foundation of our relationship is cultivated and nurtured so that we can grow into a LoveTeam.

The Buddy System

According to Wikipedia, "The buddy system is a procedure in which two people, 'the buddies,' operate as a single unit so that they are able to monitor and help each other."[30] In other words, two people care about and protect the other. Hopefully, you two consider yourselves buddies!

What are a few ways we can practice the buddy system with our partner? Physically, we can protect them from a safety standpoint. We can become aware of where they are and what they are doing, whether we're around our home or elsewhere. For instance, if when walking together we see that someone on a bicycle may hit them, we can call a warning or pull them to safety. When doing household chores that are somewhat dangerous, we can be available to offer assistance, like holding a ladder as they climb and work. Considerate teammates have a strong desire to keep their loved one safe.

A less obvious but equally important way to be their buddy is to protect them emotionally. When they're going through a difficult time, we can be the trustworthy, caring person they need. They should feel comfortable openly sharing their deepest feelings and concerns when they know we will still love them and won't share confidences with others. And we don't keep secrets from one another. In a team-building relationship, both strive to be each other's confidant and best friend.

Highest Priority

The moment we say "I do" or become a committed couple, our priorities in life change. In order to be a LoveTeam, our most important relationship must be with our mate, and our team becomes our top priority. What's best for the two of us together becomes more important than what's best for one or the other of us. Everything is evaluated by what will enhance and improve our team, and keep it going in *The LoveTeam Game Plan* direction. Whether we are making decisions about jobs, leisure activities, our energy, time, money, or anything else, our team should be foremost in our mind. If not, the unintentional results will be a splintering of our relationship.

Maintaining our LoveTeam unity takes priority over what we consider desirable for each of us individually. Being unselfish is one of the biggest factors in determining a close friendship. We must expect to give up some of ourselves, but we get so much more in return, as exemplified in a previous chapter, "The Snapshots." It will take time, effort, and a lot of communicating to determine what's best for both of us, but as decisions are made with our team in mind, life gets so much easier together.

The following are two simple examples of how we can get the focus off of ourselves:

We're hiking together and one of us gets thirsty. We can assume the other might also be thirsty, so we could offer them a drink before taking one ourselves.

When we're ready to go to bed, it's nice to find out if our mate is ready too by asking, "Are you tired?" instead of saying, "I'm tired." Or we could say something like, "I'm ready to go to bed whenever you are." This type of thinking puts the emphasis on the other person and shows team-like consideration.

There will be circumstances that must be temporarily prioritized, such as a deadline at work, a sick child, or an extended family member with an urgent need. Underlying this short-term circumstance is always the concept that our partner is still the most important person in our heart. These unusual needs of others, however, should be addressed in a healthy way for our relationship. We should be understanding of each other when situations like these happen.

Loyalty

We owe our loyalty to our partner. Relationship issues should be kept between the couple, since disclosing private matters to others could be destructive to forming a strong bond, except in extreme circumstances like physical abuse and illegal actions. When both the team and love elements are applied in our relationship, we become empowered to solve our own issues.

To get advice about personal, career, or most other matters, who better to ask than the person who is our best friend and knows us so well? When we seek advice from others, except in technical cases, our lovemate will feel they aren't valued and needed. This is a subtle form of disloyalty.

Similarly, the same is true when we need emotional support. This includes sharing triumphs, tragedies, stressful situations, grief, and the like. When an emotion-provoking situation happens, it should be an automatic reaction for a person to go to or call their lovemate. After all, they are the one trustworthy person who will understand and give them the needed support and encouragement. There may be others who will provide some secondary support, but our mate should always be our primary source of empathy, sympathy, and love.

Additionally, it's disloyal to our soulmate to make remarks about the physical qualities of someone else of the opposite sex. Some examples are movie stars, athletes, political figures, or someone in the community. Likewise, it is detrimental to be involved with pornography or anything similar. All of these situations are disrespectful to our teammate and show a lack of appreciation for the special relationship we have with each other.

Other Priorities

We can tell what our priorities are in several ways: By what we talk about the most, what we spend the majority of our time thinking and doing, and what stresses us the most. In our society, people have many different priorities. These include:

- Hobbies
- Career
- Friends
- Money
- Cars
- Sports
- Their children
- Extended family
- Addictions

- Themselves
- Their home
- Valued objects
- Pets

If a couple wants their relationship to be great, none of the above-mentioned priorities should come before their union. In the sports world they'd say, "Make your home team stronger than your away team."

In the movie *Fever Pitch*, the main character is Ben, who is the ultimate Boston Red Sox fan. He goes to nearly all their games. During the off-season, he falls in love with a woman named Lindsay and their relationship begins to develop into something special. However, when baseball season begins, his interest, time, and loyalties are centered on the Red Sox. He gives Lindsay almost no attention, unless she goes to a game with him. She ends their relationship because of his obsessive behavior. When he explains this situation to a friend, he asks Ben, "You love the Sox. But tell me, have they ever loved you back?" Guess what happens? Ben realizes where his priority has been, makes the necessary changes, and he and Lindsay resume their relationship.[31]

The Family Team

If children come along, they're blessings in our lives. They take a high place in our list of priorities. Our childrens' relationship with us should be close, especially when they're young. But the parent/child relationship is secondary to the marriage team. The couple and their children together form the second most important unit in society—the family team.

Our children will always be close to our hearts. Together we enjoy spending time and energy raising them. When they know their parents love and support each other, children feel more secure, cared for, and loved. It also gives children security knowing their parents' marriage relationship is their highest priority and provides a healthy model and perspective for their future relationships. This motivates them to look forward to a great marriage as well. (See Chapter 3, "A Wonderful Example")

If there are minor or adult children from a previous marriage, whether living in the home or not, these children need to understand that the new marriage relationship is now the couple's highest loyalty. However, the children continue to be very important because they're the couple's second priority; the blended family now forms a family team. Maturity and understanding are needed when managing these relationships, and it can be done successfully when everyone is aware of and respects the priorities.

Children will be gone from the home in eighteen years or shortly thereafter, allowing them to become independent and make a life of their own. A married couple's adult children and extended family are entitled to have their own lives, as is the couple. They can, of course, enjoy meeting together occasionally. When they do come together, they then become a larger team. It's so nice when they all think of themselves as a loving unit in which each thinks, speaks, and acts like part of an extended family team, showing concern and support for each other while still respecting the priority relationships.

When both people aren't committed to putting their relationship team first, it only takes one partner to start changing the priority. It won't be easy, but one person can begin the corrective changes that are needed. Then it's very likely that their good example will help their mate desire to do the same. It does take perseverance and time to change previously established priorities. It also takes surrounding ourselves with other people who are encouraging, supportive, and respectful of our relationship and family teams.

As a couple, we're fortunate to have a best friend and confidant with whom we can talk and share our life. They care about what we've experienced during the day and want to hear about it, and in turn we want to hear about their day as well. It gives us a chance to be the main presence in our partner's life, to share in their triumphs, and to provide empathy when needed. The rewards will be great, and our relationship will grow in ways unimaginable.

Chapter 17

Remember When

XOXO

Coming together is a beginning. Keeping together is progress. Working together is success.

~Henry Ford

Dating is a universal experience for most people in our culture because of their need for that one person who's a best friend, a soulmate, a companion for life. This is the thought that's foremost in our minds when dating—is this person the one I've dreamed about? Yes, courtship is about dreams—and excitement and romance. It's also preparation for ultimately achieving the dream of a LoveTeam relationship.

Most couples reflect on their dating experience with fond memories of fun and closeness—great times with a wonderful person by their side. A lot of the positives we remember about dating have to do with our attitudes, such as appreciating strengths, overlooking weaknesses, and giving each other the benefit of the doubt. When our relationship begins with this closeness, it should continue with even more devotion if we expand on many of the wonderful attitudes we had as we dated.

Making the Team

We actually prepare for dating prior to our first date. As a youth, we observe couples around us and think about what dating and our future relationship will be like. We make pre-dating decisions about what will be desirable in a mate and what characteristics will be disqualifiers, so that we don't waste our time dating someone we know wouldn't make a good lovemate with us. We may date several different people to gain experience and wisdom in deciding who our future lovemate should be.

This is similar to other teams. To prepare to be on an athletic team, a child might start out practicing with parents and siblings. Then they'd join a team of other children where they don't have to try out—everyone makes the team. The experience and skills they gain on these preliminary teams would then lead them to try out for a high school varsity squad—their dream. Making that team would be comparable to becoming committed to a personal relationship with someone. This is taking the first step toward becoming a LoveTeam.

A business team would also be very similar. The preparation might involve getting the appropriate education, working in the business at an entry level position, apprenticing with a mentor, and applying for a higher level job. In this example, getting hired at the higher level would be comparable to taking that first LoveTeam step.

Fortunately, we all have the freedom to choose whom we date and the opportunity to select our life-long companion. There were probably many complex reasons why you two chose each other to spend the rest of your life with. It may be a good idea now to think about the qualities your mate had, and probably still has, that you appreciated and liked in those early days.

Reflect on Your Dating Experience

At various times and in many ways, elements of team were likely present during that special time of dating. You probably decided together what time to leave for a date, what you were going to do, whether to have others join you, and many other details. You saw how they were similar to you, and if you were perceptive enough you saw how they were different. Could their strengths balance your weaknesses and thus complete you? Would they be unselfish and cooperative—attributes that are important in forming any team?

Other questions you might have been asking yourself: Did you feel comfortable communicating with them? Could you make each other happy? Did they have the values and qualities that were important to you? It was a time to observe the person you were dating, to discover if they were someone you could spend your life with.

It's an important exercise to remember our dating experiences because it helps us to appreciate the qualities about our partner that convinced us that they were the one. They are still the same person with basically the same traits. However, some of their traits we used to like may now be dormant. This might be because we don't bring these out in our relationship as we did when we were dating. Sadly, we may have stopped showing our appreciation for some of their special qualities, even becoming lackadaisical.

Here are some questions to help you recall your dating experiences:

- Why was this person special?
- What nice things did they do?
- What did you do together to have fun?
- What were your emotions when you got ready for a date?
- How important was a date with them compared to other aspects of your life?

- Did you put their needs before your needs?
- Did you put them before other people?
- Did you often feel like you were acting like teammates?
- When apart, did you think mostly about them?
- Did you attempt to be your best when you were with them?
- What did you see then that made you decide to spend your life with them?
- Did you feel they were the *prize* you wanted to win?

You did win the prize—you both did! Most likely, both of you felt very fortunate to have found each other. In all the world, it's not easy to find someone we're comfortable enough with to make a lifetime commitment. In fact, many people search years to accomplish this feat, and some never achieve it. How exciting for you both!

Making Our Team Great

Relationships never stay the same. With time, they either get better or they get worse. Most people expect to have a partnership that gets better with time—more loving, caring, selfless, and team-oriented. In such a partnership, both people enjoy each other's company, are proactive in solving differences before they become problems, and actually grow closer through adversity. The other type of relationship, where a couple is unhappy, reflects what they never expected: Their partnership gets worse with time, they seldom solve their problems, and adversity moves them further apart.

It's true that when we become committed, reality soon sets in—life changes, new situations come up, and important decisions have to be made. We know nothing ever stays the same. However, when we form team and love habits that unite us, we become even closer than when we were dating. Love should grow through the years and, when we've formed a LoveTeam, our reality is that life gets sweeter with passing time.

In addition, we know each other better as time goes on. This means there are more opportunities to strengthen our relationship, as in a gold medal winning team that spends years practicing together. As life gets more complicated, we grow stronger because we have more scenarios where we can put team concepts into action. Also, our love is given full rein to grow as a result of becoming a unified team.

Our Passion

At one time, most of us were passionate about the idea of finding the one person for us. When we were dating, our relationship was undoubtedly our top priority. We dreamed about it, talked about it, and eventually made plans for it. The beginnings of devotion, loyalty, and unselfish love were there, all of which grew as our relationship grew.

When a person has a passion, that's where the majority of their thoughts, emotions, and time will be centered. They'll research and learn as much as possible about their passion. If their passion is a person, they'll find out about their likes and dislikes, their favorite leisure activities, their choice of books, the experiences that have shaped them, their goals and dreams, and so on. How well do you know your lovemate?

When we were courting, we looked for ways to please our date, like giving little gifts, surprising them with an exciting place to spend the day together, or making their favorite meal. There were so many little things we did then that were special. We can do similar things for them now to make their day and let them know we're grateful for them.

On any day of a relationship, it *is* possible to get a fresh start. There's always the potential to renew the wonderful feelings of the dating time when we attempted to be the best we could be. Now, every day, we can appreciate and enjoy the dynamic relationship we have developed, and the difference we are each making in our partner's life.

Chapter 18

Fun and Excitement

XOXO

People who never get carried away should be.
~Malcolm Forbes

When dating, many people plan outings that are fun, tease each other like kids, and laugh at each other's jokes, among other things. One of the delights about being a LoveTeam couple is that we can still do all these things for the rest of our lives! Yes, we can still have as much fun and excitement as when we were dating—in fact, we can have much more because now we know each other so well and know what each enjoys.

Committed relationships are designed to be an extension of the lively dating time. What an advantage that our time together has been expanded and becomes even better than our courtship because we have learned how to be a LoveTeam. The closeness a couple feels when they become a loving team naturally brings out the fun and playfulness in their relationship again.

Inner Sunshine

Dr. Martin Seligman, former president of the American Psychological Association, writes about an experience he had while weeding the garden with his five-year-old daughter, Nikki, in his book, *Authentic Happiness*:

> I'm goal-oriented and time-urgent and when I'm weeding in the garden, I'm weeding. Nikki, however, was throwing weeds into the air and dancing and singing. Since she was distracting me, I yelled at her, and she walked away. Within a few minutes she was back, saying, "Daddy, I want to talk to you."
>
> "Yes, Nikki?"
>
> "Daddy, do you remember before my fifth birthday? From when I was three until when I was five, I was a whiner. I whined every day. On my fifth birthday, I decided I wasn't going to whine anymore. That was the hardest thing I've ever done. And if I can stop whining, you can stop being such a grouch."
>
> This was an epiphany for me. In terms of my own life, Nikki hit the nail right on the head. I was a grouch. I had spent fifty years enduring mostly wet weather in my soul, and the last ten years as a walking nimbus cloud in a household radiant with sunshine. In that moment, I resolved to change.[32]

Dr. Seligman is the founder of the positive psychology movement. The garden experience with his daughter was the start of his professional mission to teach people to be present and future-minded, happy and positive. When we're happy in our thoughts, it will come through in our communication with everyone, but especially with our mate.

Memories of shared fun times and closeness are wonderful to reflect on. We should learn the lessons to be taught from past negative experiences and mistakes, but they should be forgiven and forgotten. Like Dr. Seligman, we also have a chance for a fresh start every day and an opportunity to have "a household radiant with sunshine."

The following are some of our suggestions to bring fun and excitement into your lives. No doubt you both can think of many other ways to give vitality to your relationship in your own ways.

Everyday Activities Can be Fun

Tasks and chores we all do, some on a regular basis, can become mundane. We can give ourselves a challenge to make many of these things more enjoyable. It might take a little creativity, but that's half the fun. For example, if both of you are doing chores around the house, you can turn on some upbeat music and hum or sing along while you work, making something boring almost enjoyable! Or sometimes when you pass each other in the house while working, you can hug and kiss.

Routines you do together can be made more exciting with small changes your partner doesn't expect, each time a little different. For instance, when the two of you watch television, you can do different things during the commercials like dancing or exercising. When you brush your teeth, one of you can put the toothpaste on both brushes, then hand it to the other in an unexpected way—like upside down. In other words, take what's ordinary and make it extraordinary.

When you go out to eat, sometimes try new restaurants. You might even try unusual meals you wouldn't normally fix at home. We, personally, choose two different entrees that we both think we'll like, then share them so we get twice the variety. Also, when in a restaurant we find it more enjoyable to sit on the same side of a four-person booth for several reasons: we can look at the menu together, keep our conversation more private, have the same visual field, and hold hands if we want to.

In one of our favorite movies, *What About Bob?* Bob is an unusual friend of the family. The family has an important event the following day, so Bob, who shared dinner with them, makes doing the dishes fun by throwing the plates to the mother, who catches each one before placing it in the dishwasher. They're laughing and obviously having fun, no longer worrying about the next day's event.[33] We, too, can find ways to eliminate our stress and make life more fun by bringing laughter into our lives.

Just as it's important to develop enthusiasm and excitement in our relationship, constancy and predictability are also necessary. We should find the right balance between these two concepts. Have the comfort and trust necessary so that our relationship is stable, but also include some flexibility to have fun and share adventures together.

Stop and Smell the Roses

It's so important to have spontaneous, energizing times in our lives together. They don't have to be elaborate or expensive, or be planned far in advance. Hopefully, we've built some excitement into our relationship, more than just our annual vacation. Many of our most exciting memories surely are spur of the moment, whereas others are well planned and anticipated. The planning is certainly some of the fun, too.

It can be enjoyable simply walking around the block together. Think of all the *roses* you can stop and smell as you do everyday things together. Some exciting things can be done inside your own home, such as fixing and sharing an unusual meal together; holding a contest of throwing empty water bottles into a container; or learning to dance with an instructional video. Following *The LoveTeam Game Plan* will naturally enable you to have more pleasure in your lives. If neither of you is very creative, there are many resources you can access both online and in books to help you come up with fun things to do together.

Some of our many special memories include sharing a huge banana split as our lunch; hiking to the top of a nearby mountain (as well as laughing about the aches we suffered afterward); watching an armadillo cross a road when neither of us had ever seen one before; and kissing and hugging while waiting for the microwave to finish warming our meal.

Part of having fun is to be goofy and child-like at times. Life isn't meant to always be serious and solemn. Children enjoy life by being playful—they make fun out of what isn't usually fun. Being more like children at times can help us enjoy life with each other. It also reduces stress and minimizes pressures. Several people, when they've seen us holding hands and interacting together, have called us "kids." What a compliment!

When there's a reason to celebrate something, we give ourselves time to relish those moments together. As an athletic example, a basketball team has just won the conference. One player is being interviewed by a reporter on the playing floor as his teammates are celebrating behind them. The reporter asks a question about the upcoming regional tournament. Most players would reply that they would prefer to concentrate on and talk about their win of today. They would rather not think past this moment of celebration. Life becomes sweeter when we learn to appreciate the good times. As the Latin poet Horace wrote, "Seize the Day!"

Humor—Appropriate and Inappropriate

Using humor when things get too serious is a trait that can be cultivated. It isn't easy for some people, but it's not too difficult to be a little silly, make a joke, or throw a paper wad when the mood gets too somber! In other words, we *lighten up*. The right kind of humor reduces stress by releasing chemicals in the brain, called endorphins, that are good for our health. This can make a difference in enjoying life together, as well as appreciating our teammate's playfulness.

One type of light-hearted humor is when the unexpected happens, like washing the car together and getting sprayed! Be sure that the person who does the light-hearted gesture or joke gets the proper response of laughter and appreciation from the other so they're encouraged to keep doing similar things.

However, couples should be aware that some types of humor can actually reduce trust and cause disharmony. Humor in a relationship must always be "clean," well-timed, and non-discriminatory. If it's truly humor, everyone involved should feel better. Joking should never make fun of or belittle another person. The results of name-calling, put-downs, and sharing inappropriate stories can be one of the worst things that can happen for our relationship.

Couples should find the right balance between humor and seriousness in their relationship. If a person jokes when their partner thinks an important decision needs to be made, or any other time when humor just isn't appropriate, this can actually hamper their team relationship. Well timed, appropriate humor can draw a couple closer.

Some of the main things children remember about their childhood are the enjoyable and humorous times experienced within their family. With this in mind, have fun as a couple on a regular basis as well. Then, when the children all leave home, you'll be in the habit of enjoying laughter together, plus you will have set a good example.

Chapter 19

Building a Life Together

XOXO

If you want to make good use of your time, you've got to know what's most important and then give it all you've got.

~Lee Iacocca

We were at the home of a couple who had recently celebrated their sixty-fifth wedding anniversary and were very close and loving. We asked the wife when she thought that their marriage seemed like they'd formed a team. She replied that in the first few years they had to work through some difficult and frustrating times together. Then she remarked that after about ten years of marriage, she realized that when he was in another room, she missed him.

This couple had spent many, many days together over the years. It was obvious that they were in each other's hearts and minds even when they weren't physically together. According to their story, they didn't seem to have the team or possibly the love ideas from the beginning, but had certainly found them along the way. Fortunately, you don't have to just hope that you will stumble onto the system that will help you to feel the way this couple did. When you become a LoveTeam, your lives together will be similar to this couple who still seemed so much in love.

A Single, Stable Unit

High-functioning couples think of themselves as a single unit—unified in thoughts, words, and actions. When a couple functions this way, rather than as two individuals with separate agendas, their relationship gains stability and endurance.

A catamaran boat is formed from two hulls that are held side by side with a frame above them, typically propelled by a sail. Think how stable a catamaran is compared to a sailboat, which has only one hull. It's so much easier for a sailboat to capsize in bad weather than a catamaran.

Another example is the image of two high-wire walkers. If they walk several feet apart on different wires, both holding on to the same pole, their stability is so much better than if they walked holding separate poles.

Most of us have experienced other examples of solidity, such as solving a problem together, being able to depend on our partner in times of trouble, and holding hands when hiking to catch the other if they start to fall. As a couple, how do we gain stability like a catamaran or high-wire walkers? One way is to spend as much quality time together as possible.

Spend Time Together

When dating, most couples do as much together as possible, getting to know each other by talking a great deal. They may not realize it, but they are in the process of becoming a unified team. Unfortunately, over time some couples revert back to what was comfortable for them when they were single and unattached. The closeness and glamour of their dating time together is lost—that time when they began to function successfully as a team.

Many couples grow closer and closer through the years, as the previously-mentioned senior couple. Even when they were not together, their relationship continued to grow closer. In a relationship like that, couples learn to avoid anything that pulls them apart and form the habits that unite them. In this book, you are learning what may pull couples apart, what words and actions create unity, and how to become lovemates.

Everything we say and do, whether together or apart, should be showing consideration and loyalty to our mate, as if they are present. Otherwise, *we risk having an emotional or physical affair.* The following circumstances increase our chances of this happening, whether we do them intentionally or unintentionally:

- Having hobbies, activities, or interests we don't share with our mate.
- Spending more time with others than with our partner.
- Thinking more about someone who isn't our lovemate.
- Being alone with a person of the opposite sex.

Find reasons to be together with the person you love. Studies have shown that the average couple today spends twenty minutes a day, three times a week talking together. Relating this to a basketball team, we don't believe it's possible to have a successful team when the players practice mostly in different gyms, and spend only twenty minutes a day three times a week practicing together. The camaraderie among team members would be lost, or never gained.

We advise couples to spend some quality time alone together regularly, preferably away from the responsibilities of home and family. When we go out for an evening or get away for a weekend, it can bring us closer if we just concentrate on positive aspects of each other and our relationship. We can share present, future, and wonderful past experiences as we lovingly have fun and enjoy each other's company, similar to when we were dating. The good times we have will also provide memories we can talk about for the rest of our lives. If we take pictures, we can look at them later and relive our experiences, reminding us of the strong bond we share.

If we start each day spending affectionate time together, our relationship will be solidified and our day will be more successful. Also, spending the end of the day lovingly together will carry through to the next day—and, as a bonus, we will sleep better. In athletics, if a basketball team can start a game by scoring the first ten points, they have a greater chance of winning. If this same team can also finish the game with gusto by scoring a lot of points, the players become excited because they now have momentum. Couples who start and finish their day lovingly will have similar momentum in their relationship.

Interdependence

In the tennis book, *The Art of Doubles,* the writer asserts, "If you and your partner commit the time necessary to become an accomplished team, you will discover that by making things happen, you can continue to improve as long as you play the game."[34] Since committed couples have an interdependent relationship like a tennis team, the more time they spend together in harmony, the closer they'll feel to each other.

Interdependence is like a peanut butter and jelly sandwich: once you put them together, it's literally impossible to separate them back into just peanut butter and just jelly. Or think of a rope: A three-strand rope woven together is much stronger than the separated three strands.

Our society so often applauds the individual and attempts to keep a couple separate. In many circumstances, it's very difficult to be acknowledged as a couple. When applying for a credit card, when volunteering in a charity walk, when signing up for store rewards, and in so many other examples, most computers aren't programmed to enter one account in both names. One time, when we signed up with a national drug chain to get some pictures developed, we gave the clerk both of our first names, along with our last name. She told us this was the first time since working there that she had seen two first names on the same account.

Hobbies, Interests, Chores

We went to a tennis club recently to see if we wanted to join. While speaking with the manager, she described their large number of individual men's and women's tennis teams. When we told her we were only interested in the *mixed* teams (a man and a woman together), she looked surprised and asked, "Can't we separate you two?" Needless to say, we didn't join that club.

People usually have individual hobbies each has developed before they knew each other. How fun it is when our mate takes an interest in our hobbies, whether they're just supportive of us pursuing it, become our biggest fan, or actively take up the hobby with us.

Here are some examples of leisure activities that are common: One person enjoys going to the movies and the other likes to watch football; or one enjoys bowling and the other likes to play table tennis. How nice when both participate together in what each partner likes to do. Also, it can bring a couple closer when they develop a new interest or hobby together.

We can become a team in doing chores around the house and yard as well. If one mate does all or most of the tasks, they won't have as much time or energy to spend with the other later. This can become a burden *and* be a hindrance to their relationship. A couple can develop a system of doing chores that takes into consideration the strengths and preferences of each of them. Tasks then become more efficient and less trying. If both partners have an equal amount of time and energy, they can do chores simultaneously—then when they're finished they can reward themselves by doing something pleasurable together. In a great relationship, there can be a LoveTeam approach to almost everything!

Life together can be thought of as a series of adventures—some good and some not as good. But everything we see and experience is so much sweeter and enjoyable when we share it with the person we love. The time we devote to our lovemate and our relationship will reap many rewards as we grow closer through the years.

xoxo
I Love You

Chapter 20

Kindness

XOXO

As much as we need a prosperous economy, we also need a prosperity of kindness and decency.

~CAROLINE KENNEDY

Consistent acts of kindness soften the heart and help make differences melt away in a relationship. As Albert Schweitzer has noted, "Constant kindness can accomplish much. As the sun makes ice melt, kindness causes misunderstanding, mistrust, and hostility to evaporate." Every moment of our days together should reflect the loving attitude of our hearts toward each other. We shouldn't wait for a crisis to show tenderness to our partner and be attentive to their needs.

In her book, *Fascinating Womanhood*, Helen Andelin writes that in marriage:

> …our expressions are gentle, tender, sweet, with a soft look in the eyes. Facial expression has its roots in character. If you have a gentle character, it's natural

and easy to have a gentle expression. The face acts as a teacher to the character, reminding it to be patient and forgiving."[35]

Gentleness

We should naturally want to be gentle with our teammate as a result of the love we have for them. Usually it takes only one person to increase the quality and quantity of loving gestures, and the other will do the same.

John Wooden, a great college basketball coach, wrote this about his father:

> I never heard him say an unkind word about anyone. I saw my dad's gentle spirit on display when he worked with fractious horses and with dogs I thought were vicious.
>
> I remember a young man whipping a short-tempered team of horses, trying to get them to come out of a gravel pit. They were pulling against each other, jumping back and forth, fretting and stomping. My dad went to the boy and said, "Let me take 'em."
>
> He stood amongst them. He got his head between their heads as they continued sweating, fretting, and stomping. By talking to each of them and patting them, he quieted them down. Then he went behind them and took the reins, let go, and they immediately pulled out together. His gentleness made all the difference.
>
> There is nothing stronger than gentleness.[36]

This story of a father, with his son observing, was a great example of how people should treat each other. Since Wooden states that he never heard his father "say an unkind word about anyone," his father obviously treated his wife and children with kindness. In addition, his gentleness with the horses enabled them to work together as a team to climb out of the gravel pit. It's interesting that later John Wooden became known for being one of the most team-oriented and successful college basketball coaches of all time.

How many times would it take for a person to lovingly greet their mate at the door when he arrives home before he feels better toward her? How many times would it take for a person to gently rub his teammate's sore feet for her feelings toward him to improve? Not many.

Consistently doing nice things for the other, not because we expect anything in return but because we want to, will deepen our love for them. This is because it's human nature to develop a special love for those we care for. In addition, it's healthier for our relationship to do many small kindnesses frequently than to be thoughtful only occasionally, no matter how large the gesture.

Patience

There were several wonderful lessons taught to a young woman in this old Korean legend of "The Tiger's Whisker":

> Yun Ok came to the house of a wise sage for counsel. Her problem was this: "It is my husband, wise one," she said. "He is very dear to me. For the past three years he has been away fighting in the wars. Now that he has returned, he hardly speaks to me or to anyone else. If I speak, he doesn't seem to hear. When he talks at all, it is roughly. If I serve him food not to his liking, he pushes it aside and angrily leaves the room. Sometimes when he should be working in the rice

field, I see him sitting idly on top of the hill looking toward the sea! I want a potion," she said, "so he will be loving and gentle as he used to be." The wise sage told her to bring him a whisker from a living tiger, from which he was to make the magic potion.

At night when her husband was asleep, Yun Ok crept from their house with a bowl of rice and meat sauce in her hand. She went to a place on the mountainside where a tiger was known to live. Standing far from the tiger's cave she held out the bowl of food, calling the tiger to come and eat, but the tiger did not come. Each night she returned doing the same thing and each time she came a few steps closer to the tiger. Although the tiger did not come to eat, he did become accustomed to seeing her.

One night she approached within a stone's throw of the cave. This time the tiger came a few steps toward her and stopped. The two of them stood looking at each other in the moonlight. It happened again the following night, and this time they were so close she could talk to him in a soft, soothing voice. The next night, after looking carefully into her eyes, the tiger ate the food she held out for him. After that, when Yun Ok came in the night she found the tiger waiting for her on the trail.

Nearly six months passed since the night of her first visit. At last one night, after caressing the animal's head, she said, "Oh, generous animal, I must have one of your whiskers. Do not be angry with me." And she snipped off one of his whiskers.

Yun Ok ran down the trail with the tiger's whisker tightly clutched in her hand. When she brought it to the wise sage, he examined it then tossed it into the fire. "Yun Ok," said the sage, "is a man more vicious than a tiger? Is he less responsive to kindness and understanding? If your gentleness and patience can win the confidence of a wild and bloodthirsty animal, it can do the same with your husband."[37]

What Yun Ok learned and what we can learn, is that patience and kindness, even in the face of great adversity, will most certainly bring about change in a person and in a relationship. Harmony can be restored, and then prevail, where there's respectful patience and sincere kindness.

Our love means we restrain ourselves from doing or saying unkind things. If we don't, especially when doing or saying something we know bothers our partner, they may question our love. Emotions and feelings that are positive, including patience, can radiate joy to our lovemate, and our relationship will have the potential to be awesome!

Love Reciprocated

When a kindness is shown, let's return the favor by expressing appreciation or by returning the kindness, or both. As examples, when a man opens a car door for a lady, the reciprocal thing is for the lady to say, "Thank you," every time. Similarly, when one says, "I love you," the expected response is for the other to say, "I love you," or something similar back. It's important for us as loving people to reciprocate in our own way every tender expression of love.

In order to have a great relationship, negative feelings should be restrained. Keeping score or venting at each other never enhances our feelings for each other. These emotions can turn to anger and can, in fact, change a difference of opinion into a conflict. After all, no one thinks clearly when their fists are clenched, and certainly no one thinks kindly with this type of non-team attitude.

To have a truly loving partnership, it's meaningful for us to be not only kind and patient with each other—we also need to develop attributes of compassion and empathy. This is impossible unless we have a soft attitude of humility and forgiveness, knowing that *we* make mistakes and have weaknesses as well.

How often should we be nice to each other? On the first Monday of the month? Once per day? When they've been nice to us? Actually, we should be loving and kind to our partner when we start and end our day together, and all the time in-between. When both lovemates are consistently and often nice to each other, show loving care and concern, we can expect every day to seem like Valentine's Day!

Chapter 21

Affection

XOXO

Affection is responsible for nine-tenths of whatever solid and durable happiness there is in our lives.

~C. S. Lewis

The opportunity to give and receive affection on a regular basis is one of the biggest advantages we have as a couple. As Victor Hugo, a French writer, points out: "The supreme happiness in life is the conviction that we are loved." In a great team relationship, frequent loving words and gestures exchanged between the partners are happily received and reciprocated.

Only one part of affection is the physical aspect, which includes hugging, kissing, massaging, or even a soft pat on the shoulder. Affection can also be shown in other ways, such as verbally when we say, "I love you," "You are so special," or any of many similar expressions. In addition, our loving actions can be considered affectionate, such as bringing flowers to our mate, blowing them a kiss through the air, or smiling lovingly into their eyes. Showing affection says to them that we not only love and like them, but also adore and cherish them.

Skin Hunger

The skin is the largest organ in the human body, and plays a big part in affection. The term "skin hunger" is relatively new and describes the human need for touch that goes unsatisfied. Comparable to the hunger of our body for food, the hunger to be lovingly touched has dire consequences as well, if not met. From the website, Everything2:

> One of the five basic senses, touch is the only one deemed essential to human life. During WWII, babies in orphanages developed failure to thrive or even died when deprived of human contact. In a classic study by Harry Harlow, newborn monkeys were taken from their biological mothers and given surrogates made of either wire or soft terry cloth. The baby monkeys consistently chose the soft mother even when deprived of nourishment. The need for bonding outweighed even the basic necessity of food. The need for touch extends beyond the early developmental years. It is the first sense to develop in utero and the last to diminish as we die.[38]

A few of the positive effects of calm, soothing touch are reduced stress, lowered blood pressure, and raised levels of serotonin, which is a neurotransmitter in our bodies that contributes to well-being and happiness. Skin hunger, when not satisfied, can lead to depression, moodiness, anger, anxiety, pain, drug dependence, alcoholism, and other serious maladies. It's up to each of us to satisfy our lovemate's skin hunger with an abundance of affection.

Non-sexual touching is important in a relationship, as well as being an integral part of the sexual aspect, which will be covered later in this chapter. We need to know that we're cared about and loved, and realize that touching shouldn't always lead to intimacy. Zig Ziglar, motivational speaker, describes how meaningful simple hugs between spouses are:

> The hug really says, "I love you, I enjoy being around you, you're important to me, I look forward to spending more time with you." There's an old saying that actions speak louder than words, and to take a few seconds a number of times during the day to get and give those non-suggestive hugs really speaks volumes.[39]

Touch Often

William Shakespeare wrote, "They do not love that do not show their love." It's one thing to think affectionate thoughts about our mate; it's quite another to put those thoughts into action. We believe touching between partners should be multiple times a day—not just occasionally. Frequent touching may not be natural for some people who haven't been touched much in their past or seen examples of it. However, it's a behavior that can be put into practice and will feel normal, and wonderful, the more often it's done. Expressions of affection should be appropriate when considering when, how, and where we are: In public or private, in front of our children, and in what specific circumstances we're in.

If you feel uncomfortable picking up the pace of showing affection, talk to your mate. Ask what they would be comfortable with, and share your own thoughts about frequency and types of affection. It may seem awkward at first, but the benefits will far outweigh the awkwardness. Before you know it, giving and receiving more affection will feel natural, as habits do with time. After all, how bad can touching be?

What can National Basketball Association players teach us about being touchy-feely? From an article entitled, "Little Touches Make Big Impact in Relationships":

> Benedict Carey…wrote in February [2010] about research in *Mind* magazine in an article called "Evidence That Little Touches Do Mean So Much" from high-fives to warm touches on the shoulder.
>
> One research team tracked every "bump, hug, and high five in a single game played by each team in the National Basketball Association early last season." The journal, *Emotion,* is to publish the results this year, but the results are telling:
>
> + Good teams tended to have more touches than bad ones.
> + The league's top two teams were the most touch-bonded teams—the Boston Celtics and the Los Angeles Lakers.
> + The least touchy teams were the Sacramento Kings and Charlotte Bobcats, neither of which had good seasons.[40]

Later in the same article it said that researchers also studied couples, and they noted that those who touched more during the interviews reported the highest satisfaction in their relationship.

Here are a few suggestions for increasing the affection in your relationship:

+ Kiss each other when leaving from and arriving home.

- Come up behind your partner when they're doing something and hug them or scratch their back.
- Touch them when they are talking about their day.
- Hold hands whenever appropriate, such as sitting in a theater.
- Hug for longer than a minute the first thing in the morning and the last thing at night.
- Cuddle close when watching television on your *love*seat!
- Offer to give back rubs and to massage sore muscles.

There are times when the caring touch of a loved one becomes vitally important. These include before going into major surgery, when one finds out they have cancer, or when there's a tragedy. The loving touch and affection of our soulmate means more than words can express.

Pillow Talk

We'll now briefly discuss a few of the sexual aspects of relationships. For a comprehensive study, there are other books that cover this subject in more detail.

Intimacy reflects our emotional, mental, and physical state of mind as a couple and as individuals. Since satisfying sex is mainly a result of good communication, it's important to get to know the other and learn what they like and don't like in this important area. We, then, know how we can please them, inside the bedroom and out. This is essential because sex doesn't just stay in the bedroom—it affects our overall relationship. If there are any concerns, they'll need to be discussed together and solved.

Stresses of the day and differences of opinion should be kept out of the bedroom. This is a couple's private play area. It's important to know that when we're having difficulties, whether they're issues that involve our relationship or anything else, intimacy is usually adversely affected. Therefore, we see that there's a direct correlation between how our relationship is going and the state of our sex life. When either isn't going well, both aspects are affected.

When a couple is observed being appropriately affectionate in a public setting, many people will ask them, "How long have you two been married?" What they're assuming is that the couple hasn't been married long. This doesn't have to be the case, though, because showing affection shouldn't diminish with time. When couples are newly committed, affection is the natural response to the bonding that's taking place. Fortunately when a couple is a LoveTeam, this same bonding, and thus affection, will keep growing through the years. Could life be sweeter than this?

Chapter 22

Appreciation

XOXO

Gratitude is not only the greatest of virtues, but the parent of all others.

~Cicero

When you first got to know your partner, what traits about them interested you? What was it about them that influenced you to decide they were the person with whom you wanted to spend the rest of your life? It's true that we didn't know everything about them early on, but we knew their major characteristics. Those traits were acceptable to commit to a lifetime with them.

Even though we've already chosen our lovemate, we still have many choices to make in our lives together. One choice is how we determine to look at things. Ask yourself this question—the majority of the time do you have an attitude of being grateful? Dwelling on our mate's good traits, and appreciating what's good about our lives will go a long way toward achieving happiness. It's so much better to be thankful and to let the good things register much more highly than the negative. As Abraham Lincoln noted, "We'd all be much happier if we magnified our blessings rather than our disappointments."

Tap into the Positives

We appreciate only what we perceive as positive. For fun, we recommend that you play a game together called "The Alphabet Game." When the two of you can find some quiet time, take turns expressing a good quality about each other, starting with the letter *A*, such as "adorable." Then do the same with the letter *B*, and so forth, using the complete alphabet. (It's okay to be silly.) It may take several sessions, but persevere all the way to the letter *Z*. At the end you both will surely have learned a few things, had fun, but especially will have renewed your appreciation of each other.

There may be a time when one of you is affected by a temporary bad situation such as a health issue, a job layoff, or loss of a sibling. The other then has an opportunity to be understanding and empathetic, and to make adjustments so your LoveTeam becomes stronger. Similarly, the affected partner should show their appreciation for the effort and caring of their lovemate, and reciprocate the favor later in their own way. The relationship becomes an even better and stronger team in spite of these difficult occurrences.

The above situations, those we have no control over, aren't the same as personality traits or habits that *can* be changed. When our mate is willing to work on a habit that is hindering our relationship, we need to appreciate their effort to improve the team, knowing it's not easy and that they'll need encouragement. On the other hand, when the other has a trait that isn't team-oriented and they aren't willing to change it, our best response is to concentrate on their good qualities and show them love in spite of this weakness.

It's important to let our soulmate know when they do something we appreciate. By verbally expressing words of gratitude, it helps them know what we like. By telling them specifically what they've said or done that has positively impacted us, they'll most likely be motivated to keep doing it, and we can then reciprocate by doing things they like.

Voltaire said, "Appreciation is a wonderful thing. It makes what is excellent in others belong to us as well." This is especially true in a relationship because we both understand the power of the other's strengths in making our team more complete, and in a way we inherit their strong points—how fortunate!

Worthy of Appreciation

When we think about what we're grateful for in our partner, superficial attributes like outward appearance or intelligence (IQ) are essentially unimportant. Appreciating a person's inner values is so much more meaningful because these are traits they've purposely developed; they weren't born with them. Several examples of personal values and habits worthy of appreciation are:

- Their unselfish acts when they're kind, affectionate, and considerate
- Their wisdom gained by maturity
- The things they do to make the world better
- Their forgiving nature
- Their willingness to do difficult or mundane tasks
- Their desire to learn new things
- The time they spend with the family
- Their work ethic and worthy goals
- Their courage and honesty
- Their sacrifices

When someone appreciates our inner values, it's so much more fulfilling to us. Since we know each other so much better than anyone else, we have the opportunity to give meaningful appreciation. This is generally easy for lovemates to do and will have a big impact on our relationship.

Our Focus

If we put our teammate above all else and don't take them for granted, it will be easier to appreciate them. Focusing on their good points is a mental exercise we can get into a habit of doing, and without a doubt they will appreciate our appreciation!

In the book, *The Complete Idiot's Guide to the Perfect Marriage*, the authors write:

> Most couples let a lot of time go by without letting one another know how much they care about each other. They treat their relationship as one more ordinary thing in their lives. Their obligations all run together; projects at work, catching up on bills, getting dinner on the table, and being in a marriage.
>
> Don't take your most important relationship for granted. If you want your relationship to be extraordinary, you can't throw it in with all the ordinary things you have to do every day. You want your marriage to be much more than just another daily obligation.
>
> ...If you are always thinking of your spouse and doing things for him or her, it's impossible to take your relationship for granted. And you'll be keeping it fresh and exciting at the same time.[41]

Some people fall into the aforementioned habit of taking each other for granted. Couples may think their partner will always be there for them no matter what, so they don't exert much effort or give much time to their relationship. However, we don't know what tomorrow will bring, and we don't want to have any regrets. Thus, it becomes not just a nice thing to do, but very important to be grateful for our lovemate and to let them know we appreciate them. Let's make every day count.

Chapter 23

Respect

XOXO

Time is not so short but that there is always time for courtesy.
~Ralph Waldo Emerson

When two people marry or become committed to each other, their respect level for each other is normally very high. Most people wouldn't choose someone they didn't respect or think respected them. This high regard is felt by the tender tones of our voice when speaking, the admiration in our eyes, and our desire to understand. Unfortunately, these are some of the responses that couples may lose over the years.

Think of being an employee of a company. To show respect for your fellow employees, you do your job to the best of your ability so the others don't have to fill in for your incompleteness. Also, you treat each of them with respect and appreciation so that the mood in the office stays positive. After all, you spend forty hours a week with them! Hopefully, it's easy to see the correlation between being a respectful employee and having these same attitudes at home with our mate.

Respect Quiz

Ask yourself the following questions related to respect:

- When both of you are talking to friends, do you treat your partner's opinions with as much, or more, regard than your friends'?
- Are you on time when you're both going somewhere together, and are you punctual when you meet them for appointments?
- Do you confer with them in most decisions, considering both opinions?
- Do you concentrate on their strengths and minimize their weaknesses?
- Do you remember their birthday and other special events?
- When your partner has something important happening at work, do you remember to ask about it when they get home?
- Do you put a high value on the other's relatives?

How did you do? Did you get more yes answers than no's? And are there improvements you could make? Hopefully this quiz will help you become more aware of some common situations in the very important area of respect.

When our mate has more experience and knowledge in a subject, they become the leader in this area. As we make decisions together in these cases, we should trust their suggestions based on respect for their expertise. They'll feel our consideration and appreciation by our show of confidence in their opinions. We, in turn, will be richly rewarded with their increased love and devotion.

There may be times when a partner does something that lowers the level of respect felt by the other. It's important to forgive, continue to have confidence, be encouraging, and believe they will again meet agreed-on team expectations. This should eventually bring them back up to a level where they again deserve the other's utmost respect. Ideally, our esteem for each other continues to grow with time.

In a great relationship, respect doesn't continually have to be earned—it's automatic. That's because we value this person higher than any other in the world, and they need to know that. When we give them the benefit of the doubt, we are allowing for occasional mistakes. Let's look for opportunities to show respect and admiration for each other.

Courtesy

Oliver Wendell Holmes so aptly said, "Don't flatter yourself that friendship authorizes you to say disagreeable things to your intimates. The nearer you come into relation with a person, the more necessary do tact and courtesy become."

People generally use their best manners with those they highly respect. Many people are subconsciously more courteous to those people they don't know very well (guests, acquaintances, and even strangers) than their lovemate. That's possibly because these less familiar people haven't proven they don't deserve it. However, our partner deserves our highest courtesy and regard by the very fact that we chose them out of all the other people in the world to be our lifetime companion.

Courteous, unselfish acts should be rewarded with a "thank you," a kiss or another loving gesture. It's so nice when one is polite to the other; we should make a point to acknowledge and appreciate what they do. Saying "please" when asking for something is one way of showing that we don't take them for granted.

Another courtesy we can extend to our mate is to be in the same room to talk to them instead of speaking (or yelling) from another room. They deserve that attention, even if it does require a few extra steps. By doing this, it will indicate that we honor and value them.

Compliments

A compliment is an expression of praise, commendation, or admiration. Sadly, according to a British survey of 2,000 men and women, compliments dropped from three per week to one per week in the first three years of marriage.[42] There's no reason why this needs to be the case.

We suggest sincerely complimenting our lovemate daily—freely and genuinely. This can do so much to enhance a relationship, reduce negativity, and lower stress. We can be on the lookout for aspects of our teammate's personality and demeanor that we like, and tell them specifically what we appreciate about them.

Hara Estroff Marano, Editor-at-Large of the magazine, *Psychology Today*, writes:

> Compliments are little gifts of love. They are not asked for or demanded. They tell a person they are worthy of notice. They are powerful gifts. But compliments work only if they are sincere reflections of what we think and if they are given freely and not coerced. Compliments backfire if they are not genuine. And faux flattery is usually highly transparent. A false compliment makes the speaker untrustworthy; it raises

suspicions about motives. And that can undermine a whole relationship.[43]

You can use the following examples of loving compliments to create sincere ones of your own: "I'm so glad I found you." "You're the best thing that ever happened to me." "Thank you for being such a great listener." "I'm so glad we're best friends."

Think of the impact of putting the simple suggestions in this chapter into practice in your relationship. Out of small things big things can happen. The big things that can happen when we show deserved respect, courtesy, and admiration toward the most important person in our life can sometimes switch a failing relationship to a whole different track—where love and team combine to equal greatness.

xoxo

Relating to Each Other

Chapter 24

What Makes Us Tick?

XOXO

Life is to be enjoyed, not endured.
~Gordon B. Hinckley

How well do we know our teammate? Usually when a couple is dating they ask a lot of questions, partly to get acquainted and partly to see if there's a disqualifier. In our own experience of dating, we made lists of each other's family members, food likes and dislikes, and previous jobs in an effort to get to know each other better. This way we each had a bigger picture of the person we were dating.

However, for most of the couples reading this book, the decision who to choose has already been made. So the important thing at this stage is to make sure we know each other well. Why is this important? By understanding the other, we then know how to respond to them better, to give individualized empathy, and to help our team function like a well-oiled machine. In other words, "In a great marriage, as part of a team, you need to take care of your partner as much as you take care of yourself," as stated by the authors of *The Complete Idiot's Guide to the Perfect Marriage*.[44]

Perception

It's not easy to see the world through another's eyes, but this quality is essential in forming a great relationship. Let's face it though—our partner is weird! Okay, so maybe they aren't really weird, they're just different. They haven't had the same experiences we've had, don't have the same background, and probably haven't formed the same opinions. Therefore, it becomes important for each of us to understand the other's point of view so we can appreciate their different opinions, and reduce the chances of conflict.

Recently we were in a store ordering a few photo prints to be developed. One of us was sitting down and the other was standing up looking at the same computer screen. The one standing kept wanting to lighten the pictures, while the one sitting kept wanting to darken them. The one sitting finally got up to stretch, and noticed, from a standing vantage point, that the pictures all looked darker when they were standing up. It took getting into the standing person's position to understand why things looked so different! The difference was all in the perception.

Have you ever driven together in a car on a sunny day and had the sun shining on only one of you? The partner without the sun on them would most likely wonder why the other wanted to have the air conditioner on. Since they were perfectly comfortable without air conditioning, they could only understand their mate's actions if they could put themselves in the other's place.

Let's say a couple goes on a vacation together. While experiencing many events and unusual circumstances, they talk about them. It may surprise the couple to discover that each person's perception of basically the same thing may be quite different. It's fun to share with someone else to enhance our experiences—thus creating twice the enjoyment. How exciting that our view of the world can be enlarged by our lovemate!

Become Proactive

When giving someone driving directions, we're only helpful if we are aware of the person's starting point. Likewise, understanding where our teammate is coming from is so important. When we write a term paper, the first step is to do research. Then we begin the process of writing the paper. Thus, by spending time with our mate and asking questions, both of which are comparable to doing research, we get to know them better so that the "process" of life together is smoother.

There are basically two ways to live a life together: Reactive and Proactive. The first, being reactive, is to respond mostly to negative events and what we disagree about. This is trial-and-error where we don't make things happen, we let things happen. The couple plods along showing little interest in knowing their mate well, and they keep doing things that are not conducive to their combined well-being. Making decisions that are best for their team is difficult and usually doesn't happen. As a result, they spend their time and emotions resolving conflicts that never had to happen in the first place. This isn't a recommended way to live our lives together.

A more preferable way to live is being proactive by applying *The LoveTeam Game Plan*. The first step in this process is knowing each other very well. This, of course, takes communication and quality time together where we learn about each other, become aware of what makes the other tick, and gain respect for their point of view. Through the years, LoveTeam couples continue to discover new aspects of each other, since we're all very complicated as well as interesting. As they increase in their knowledge of each other, they can make better decisions about what's best for their team, make plans around what they've decided, and put these plans into action—thus *avoiding* conflict.

This process is similar to a winning athletic team. The players know their teammates' strengths and weaknesses because they've spent a lot of time practicing and playing games together. They've talked and asked questions, studied each others' skills and attitudes and so can see things from the others' perspective on and off the court. These beginning steps are always present in a team that is successful.

Mutual Understanding

Becoming familiar with our soulmate (which is a life-long process), leads to understanding. Stephen Covey in his book, *The 7 Habits of Highly Effective Families,* explains:

> Try to remember a time when you had the wind knocked out of you and were gasping for air. At that moment, did anything else matter? Was anything as important as getting air? That experience demonstrates why seeking to understand is so important. Being understood is the emotional and psychological equivalent of getting air, and when people are gasping for air—or for understanding—until they get it, nothing else matters. Nothing.
>
> Next to physical survival, our strongest need is psychological survival. The deepest hunger of the human heart is to be understood, for understanding implicitly affirms, validates, recognizes, and appreciates the intrinsic worth of another. When you really listen to another person, you acknowledge and respond to that most insistent need.[45]

Why is mutual understanding so important in relationships? A deep and sincere desire to know and understand our partner better leads to a closer relationship. Yes, our mate is different, but we've already learned in a previous chapter that differences are good because, as a couple, we complete each other. When we not only accept, but also respect and appreciate their point of view, it's easier to understand.

Mutual understanding requires a willingness to see things from the other's perspective, giving them our mental and physical attention, and knowing that they are more important than anyone else. We should have respect for their beliefs, feelings, likes, dislikes, and what motivates them, among other things. When we understand them, we can encourage them to be their best. This encouragement is a way to show that we honor and love this wonderful person at our side, and that we prize the relationship we have together.

Empathy

It's a cop-out to say we can't understand one another, because we can! It takes spending time together, asking questions, listening intently, and sharing ourselves. Understanding another person leads to empathy, which is the identification of the feelings, thoughts and attitudes of another, as well as the willingness to respond to that person's needs.

Charles G. Morris, a psychology professor, confirms that "Empathy depends not only on one's ability to identify someone else's emotions, but also on one's capacity to put oneself in the other person's place and to experience an appropriate emotional response." When our teammate shares their emotions with us, it's important to show them that we respect and value what they're sharing. And we should avoid offering unsolicited solutions or advice, which can be counterproductive when giving empathy.

There are several steps that help in developing empathy and compassion. First, listen without interrupting. Second, imagine what they might be thinking—put yourself in their shoes. Third, let them know, verbally and non-verbally, that you understand. Fourth, offer support and encouragement. Fifth, if asked, offer suggestions, but only as a way to help them.

As an example of empathetic understanding, a couple is watching a movie together. The husband knows his wife doesn't like to hear profanity, but he notices this occurring repeatedly in the movie. He offers to turn off the television before she has to ask, knowing she's probably uncomfortable. He has put himself in her place.

As we see things from our partner's perspective and sympathize with their feelings, attitudes, and ideas, we can sincerely show concern for their well-being and happiness. Most people can discern if someone is being genuine or when they're just going through the motions, especially a lovemate who knows the other so well. Sincerity is much appreciated from the person who is the most important in our lives.

Proactively discovering the awesome person we chose, and developing understanding and empathy helps us to be thankful for them. Also, being in a committed relationship aids in becoming a better person because we have the opportunity to develop these enriching characteristics, which are important for any relationship, but essential in a LoveTeam.

Chapter 25
Communication

XOXO

*No man is an island entire of itself; every man is
a piece of the continent, a part of the main.*

~John Donne

It's true that once something is said, we can't press a delete button—we can't take back anything we've said. By learning to weigh the things we're going to say to our mate, we'll usually be speaking only what is good for our team and what is loving for our relationship. And "never shout when a whisper is enough," as stated in *The Art of Doubles*.[46] In addition, people have a need to be emotionally interdependent so the more communication the better.

It's been said that silence is deafening. Giving feedback is the other half of a conversation. When two are speaking and there's no acknowledgment from the one who is "listening," a clear message is sent. The message is usually not one of support and encouragement, but of disagreement or apathy. Apathy is an uncaring attitude, a lack of interest—just the opposite of how a person should respond who is in a LoveTeam partnership.

Openness

In a close, personal relationship, it's important that both people want to communicate with each other. Someone needs to make an effort to start a conversation, but it shouldn't always be the same person. In his book, *Romancing the Home*, Ed Young acknowledges:

> Good communication in marriage begins with desire. Both must begin with the desire to share with one another in a way that is open and honest and vital and real. People like to do the things that they are naturally good at; they gravitate toward them, and enjoy them. The things that are more difficult tend to be avoided, but no one can afford to avoid cultivating intimate communication with a mate, whether it comes easily or not.[47]

We should have transparent communication in almost all topics, keeping in mind that there may be a few hot-button subjects that need to be brought up only at the right time and in the best way, or in rare cases, not at all. Communicating with empathy and consideration toward our mate is important.

When we open ourselves up to the other we take risks, which are necessary to get the closeness and the acceptance we desire. We risk that what they learn about us they may not like. Or we may discover that they feel differently than we do and this might lead to difficulties. However, if a couple fails to communicate, they jeopardize their relationship because one or both of them may confide in a third party.

Unfortunately, some couples believe that being in a committed relationship is so complex that they don't open up to each other, deciding that the less time they spend talking the fewer issues they'll have. Yet, *this may lead to isolation* where the couple will find themselves leading separate lives. Thus, they won't be the support person for their mate in their time of need, have the companionship of a soulmate, or have many of the other wonderful advantages of a LoveTeam.

A Safe Haven

Communicating is a very personal thing for each couple. We develop consideration for our lovemate as we get to know them better. When they tell us their hurts, their faults, their secrets, their troubles and delights, we want to keep their confidences and let them know they have a safe haven in us.

The safe haven concept can be carried one step further. We recommend finding a place in your home, usually the bedroom, where the communication is kept *safe*—loving and personal. In other words, there should be only uplifting discussions in your safe place between the two of you. Discussions could include your appreciation for each other, loving actions noticed, upcoming events you will share, and memories of good times. When working toward cooperative solutions related to household, financial, work-related issues and the like, it's typically better not to do this in your safe place.

A safe haven such as this would give you both something to look forward to at the end of a long, complicated day. You would know that the moments spent together in your bedroom would be a place to be uplifted and reminded of your special bond, a daily renewing of your caring relationship. It would also provide an environment that's more conducive to loving habits and intimacy.

Communication Tips

Simple, daily interchanges between partners can be a highlight of their day. From an article in *Prevention Magazine:*

> "How was your day?" Asking your spouse this simple question every night can improve your relationship, says psychologist Angela Hicks, PhD, of Westminster University. She studied forty-eight couples and found that those who discussed recent positive events with each other felt happier the next day, with increased feelings of intimacy and connection to their partners. And don't be afraid to recount the low points—that discussion fostered closeness as well, Hicks says.[48]

Everyone needs a sounding board at times. Whether we're just wanting to get another opinion, are dealing with a stressful time at work, or any other situation, it's so nice to bounce our ideas and problems off someone special. There are times when we just need to talk about something to be able to solve it, knowing there's someone listening who cares about us. Our teammate is the perfect person to have as a sounding board. Thus, we should always be alert to their verbal and non-verbal cues so we can let them know we are available.

In a great relationship, rather than expect the other person to always have to communicate what they want, we could proactively meet their needs before they ask. Non-verbal ways of communicating can be as effective as verbal, such as with body language, facial expressions, or in another agreed-upon way, like lightly squeezing each other's hand as a signal. However, if we want to be sure the other understands, it would be best to communicate verbally.

When we're both conversing with someone else, we should look at our mate when they're talking, even though we know what they're going to say or we've heard it many times already. In doing this, we're showing the same courtesy to them as we would to any other person who is talking.

There's an art to listening, and it's an art that's easy to learn. Becoming a good listener has implications that can dramatically improve a relationship. There are many resources for learning the art of good listening. A few important highlights are the following:

- Give our partner our undivided attention when they're talking to us by making eye contact whenever possible, especially when we sense it's something important.
- Be sure we understand what they're telling us and, if not, ask for clarification.
- Concentrate on what they're saying and don't let our thoughts take us away to another place or time, or think only of what we're going to say next.
- Listen thoughtfully and attentively.
- If we know our lovemate has something to discuss but it's not a good time for us, set a specific time later to discuss it and then follow through.

When we make a mistake by doing or saying something we're sorry about, it's best to acknowledge it as soon as possible. Rather than say nothing at all and hope our partner doesn't notice, we can apologize and determine not to do it again. Then when they show support for our determination, it encourages us to avoid making the same mistake again.

When one person seems to make a mistake, we both should look at it from a positive standpoint—how we can use the misstep as a way to grow together. By lovingly expressing how we see their mistake and how it affects the success of our team, appropriate action can be taken. Our attitude should be one of pointing out the error *only* out of concern for the benefit of our partnership, and for the improvement of our relationship.

Couples usually develop their own working communication systems: Some may have only spontaneous discussions to meet their conversing needs, while others may set aside a regular time to talk; certain couples will prioritize their communication time by not being interrupted, while others may allow for interruptions.

Nancy Lieberman, a former professional basketball player and coach in the WNBA, wrote in *Playbook for Success* that it takes "open and honest, proactive and positive communication—the most crucial component for winning as a team."[49] As this relates to relationships, we don't necessarily want to win anything, but hopefully we do want to be the best communicating LoveTeam possible—which would mean we will be winners!

Chapter 26

Cooperative Solutions

It is through cooperation, rather than conflict, that your greatest successes will be derived.

~Ralph Charrell

We may make 100 or more big or small decisions in a day, individually or with someone else. Therefore, it's important to assess early in a relationship what decisions can be made singly and which ones need to be made together. To keep a household running and to have organization and peace, agreement is necessary. We may need to decide what to do for the weekend, what time to go to bed, what color to paint the living room, and so on. However, other decisions will obviously be more challenging. This chapter will be a general help to you in making decisions and solving concerns, especially the difficult ones that may seem unsolvable.

Almost no one chooses to commit to someone they don't like or enjoy being around. Couples were obviously resourceful enough to work through differences and avoid conflict in their dating relationship. Each couple reading this and then applying the team and love concepts in this book, should become resourceful enough to repeat the positive dating patterns of cooperative solutions. They know themselves better than anyone else, and they know the background, precedents, facts, and history of their relationship better than any outside source.

There are many complex situations that need to be decided and solved through the years. It's helpful to remember that out of the thousands of experiences and decisions a couple shares, usually only a small number lead to seemingly unsolvable problems.

Frame of Mind

Nearly all things that affect the team should be open to discussion. In most cases, it's advisable to talk as soon as possible about something that needs to be discussed because waiting too long can make it difficult to remember the details. Consideration for our teammate's frame of mind, their mental attitude, should guide us when beginning any discussion about solving a potential problem or making a decision.

Keep irritations and frustrations to a minimum since little annoyances can affect a couple's ability to solve differences in a loving way. In addition, it's not advisable to get into a complicated discussion when either one of us is tired, when it has been an emotionally trying day, or if there are strong feelings of any kind that could hinder the mood. Discussions that are initiated at such times usually don't have an ideal outcome.

After starting a discussion, if negative emotions begin to arise the conversation should temporarily stop. Then there could be a mutual "time-out" until both are in the right frame of mind, as in sports when a team is under pressure. The talk should only be continued when emotions are back under control.

When wanting to discuss anything with our mate, always consider the timing. It's usually better not to bring up a topic when we know we won't have time to complete the discussion. As examples, we wouldn't want to bring up a subject such as an ongoing parenting issue just as they are leaving for work. And we wouldn't introduce a complicated financial topic if our partner has a one-hour business deadline. In order to remember what we want to discuss, we could write down some of the key points as a reminder for a later discussion.

Differing Viewpoints

Conflicts are not to be expected in a LoveTeam, but it is normal to have different ideas and views. In fact, it's impossible for a couple to have all the same opinions and beliefs. Realizing we'll always have some differing viewpoints allows each of us to lovingly and freely voice our thoughts. The long term result is mutual understanding. In such an atmosphere, we can equally make the best team decisions.

When there's a difference between the partners, it's best to approach it respectfully with an open mind—not selfishly, defensively, or stubbornly. Both teammates should patiently explain their perspective of the situation and be willing to understand the other's point of view. In addition, when we have a team mindset of managing the present and planning for the future, we don't bring up the past unless we're sure it can lend to finding the best solution.

Differences not handled with a LoveTeam approach can lead to conflict and disharmony. If this happens, our soulmate can actually become our adversary. Teammates on an athletic, business, or personal relationship team are never successful when they feel they are on opposing sides.

As we've said, there will always be differences when two people come together. In fact, two differing ways of looking at the same thing should be welcomed because that's how growth and completion will occur. When both partners are encouraged to lovingly (a key word here) express their thoughts, and are open and willing to take each other's perspective into consideration, then productive resolutions can take place.

Seek Consensus

Consensus is defined as a general agreement; a group solidarity in sentiment and belief. Someone once said, "Teamwork is the fuel that allows common people to attain uncommon results." Consensus is an uncommon result if people aren't familiar with teamwork and aren't practicing it. We can get consensus every time if we're *a loving couple who thinks, speaks, and acts like a team.* In other words, we both need to believe and follow *The LoveTeam Game Plan* when working through differences.

A partner in a great relationship knows that no longer can joint decisions be made based solely on their individual preferences. Couples work for consensus in decision-making, and always engage in win/win strategies to come to an agreement. Several examples are: If one partner wants to invite someone over for dinner, they should have decided ahead of time if it's necessary to check with the other first. When deciding together on large purchases, such as buying a car, considerations of each partner may be taken into account. Parenting decisions usually are a joint effort whenever possible.

Many people feel that compromise is the best way to handle differing viewpoints when, in fact, it usually is not. You've heard people say that their health is *compromised,* or that a person's principles have been *compromised*—neither of which are good. Compromise is an *easy* way to solve an issue, yet generally it leaves both people unsatisfied, so therefore, is not the best conclusion. In almost all cases, if there's enough discussion with all reasons given for differing opinions, a couple can cooperatively and creatively come to a consensus that will satisfy both of them and be the best decision at that time. The key is that neither person selfishly or stubbornly pushes to get their way at the expense of their team.

Compromise is usually unsatisfactory because the team may lose out as to what is really best. But when reaching a consensus, both people have given their ideas and the decision was acceptable enough that both supported it—win/win. Compromise is, too often, a lose/lose or a win/lose decision—not desirable for what is best for a couple.

Making Decisions Together

Vince Lombardi so aptly said, "People who work together will win, whether it be against complex football defenses, or the problems of modern society." Some important factors to keep in mind when making joint decisions are to brainstorm all ideas, weigh the advantages and disadvantages, and lovingly use a team approach. Be aware that a decision that's best for the couple may not be what either of them would have decided if they were doing it individually. After a decision is made, if a new factor becomes known the decision can be reevaluated and possibly changed.

Only when decisions are made with all known facts and input given by both partners can the best conclusion be drawn. When making a decision about something that will be repeated throughout their lives, couples need to take the necessary time to discuss it, no matter how minor an issue. If it's not resolved it may become an irritation later, possibly leading to conflict or separate lives.

When brainstorming solutions, think creatively—outside the box. Write down all the possibilities if necessary. After everything is brought to the forefront and each person has lovingly given all their ideas, then, and only then, should a joint decision be made. In coming up with the best possible solution, the deciding factors should be what's best for their team, not individual preferences. A few examples of minor decisions that may be useful that could help a couple to avoid later irritation: which way to turn twisty-ties on storage bags, who gets to hold the remote control, and who will take out the trash.

If one person makes the majority of the decisions, the solution is always going to be incomplete—a "what if" situation. What if they had the additional information their mate could contribute? Seldom is this the best outcome for the couple. "What ifs" usually turn into regrets later on. Similarly, if one person always *wins* a discussion, the other will lose their desire to express their opinions or ideas, and resentment may start to build. Relationships can't be successful in either type of atmosphere.

When we aren't happy about something in our relationship, instead of just sharing our thoughts, first come up with one or more possible solutions that could be acceptable. These other options should then be brought up when the situation is shared so it doesn't seem like just a complaint session.

It's also very important to be aware that some subjects are hot-button topics; these take special handling such as the right timing, extra patience, more understanding, and motivation by both to solve it. If not handled correctly, they can quickly turn into conflict. Hot-button topics should be carefully weighed if and when to discuss them.

How many times has our lovemate helped us to avoid a personal dilemma because they've been there to help in making a decision? Many insurance companies require a second opinion when considering whether to approve a surgery or other costly medical procedure. Two heads *are* better than one, so we should be so grateful that our lovemate provides our own built-in second opinion.

After deciding on a course of action, we should stay with that direction, thereby showing confidence in the conclusion. Questioning a joint decision later can lead to uncertainty and mistrust of future decisions. Only if new facts emerge should the decision be discussed again and possibly adjusted. Every time we reconcile our differences and have consensus, we can say, "Our team won!"

Handling Adversity

Adversity can show itself in many ways: financial pressures, health conditions, death of a loved one, loss of a job, difficult adjustments in retirement, someone or something coming between us, disappointments, disasters, an affair, and others. A wise person once said, "Life isn't about waiting for the storm to pass; it's about learning to dance in the rain." Every couple has a lot invested in each other—time, emotions, love, confidences. When adversity strikes, we hope we have invested enough so that when the storm has passed, we end up stronger than ever.

There's a belief by certain people that it's better to stay in one's comfort zone; in other words, to avoid adversity and hope to go through life without any troubles or tragedies. In a like way, many parents think the best way to raise children is to shelter them from any and all problems, so they rescue them from many situations. This inhibits their child from gaining strength of character. Unfortunately, the parents learn this sad fact when their children develop problems later on.

Most people want to stay in their comfort zones. However, adversity will happen to everyone. Without adversity, there would be little growth, perseverance would not be built, and a couple wouldn't develop strength in their relationship. In actuality, we should welcome the tough times that naturally happen in life. In sports, people refer to this toughening up as intestinal fortitude or use the expression, "Get some guts."

We hear about soldiers who serve in a war zone together. They may start out in boot camp, face strict leaders, extend their energy and physical stamina nearly to the breaking point, and side by side learn that they can handle difficult situations. Then when they get into active combat where their lives are on the line, their team pulls together, supporting each other through extreme danger. What happens to their team relationship? They become very close. What this military example illustrates is that when people can handle minor adversities together, it's easier to handle larger trials.

Put yourselves in the following extreme situation and imagine how your LoveTeam would handle it: One of you leaves the door open to the swimming pool and your child drowns. This is certainly a terrible, worst-case scenario, but this type of thing does happen. The National Safety Council reports that over 90 percent of couples get divorced after such a tragedy.[50] Our relationship needs to be strong enough so that even such a terrible calamity wouldn't pull us apart. In fact, the opposite would happen. We would forgive and draw closer to each other for the emotional support that would be so necessary.

Proactive Preparation

How can you get to the point where the above tragic situation would actually bring you closer together? Becoming a LoveTeam can proactively prepare you for inevitable trials that will occur in life. If you don't feel like loving teammates now, you may need to give your relationship the necessary time to develop as you use this book for guidance. When we develop a plan *before* adversity happens, we have more assurance that we will have the strength we need to get through it as a loving team.

Teammates who are proactive can continue to grow stronger, instead of engaging in "crisis management," where they put out one fire after another. That inevitably weakens any team. Tailgaters are crisis management drivers. They obviously don't think about what would happen if the driver in front of them suddenly put on their brakes. Similarly, is just reacting to a crisis without being prepared ahead of time the best way to handle adversity?

Here's a possible scenario: A couple is just getting home from the doctor where they were told that one of them has cancer. A few minutes later, a neighbor knocks on their door. Because neither of them knows yet how the other is feeling, and until they have time to sort out this emotionally-charged news together, they don't answer the door. They are dealing with this situation proactively—they are preventing the difficulty that could ensue if they had to speak to their neighbor at this time, since obviously they need time alone together.

When adversity does strike, we need to make the necessary adjustments. Usually adversity causes very strong emotions, so we should reach out to the other by spending more time together, sharing our thoughts and feelings, canceling activities, and possibly even avoiding answering the door or phone. *Mainly realize we need our best friend during this difficult time.*

The earlier in a relationship a couple successfully navigates trials, the sooner they will feel like a cohesive, loving team. In other words, accept that you'll have difficult times; learn to bounce back from challenges, or rebound as they say in basketball. Don't dwell on missing a basket—get right back into the game and rise to the occasion.

Some proactive safeguard tips for handling adversity:

- ✦ Move closer together, both emotionally and physically.
- ✦ Show love, empathy, and compassion for one another.
- ✦ Know your team and follow *The LoveTeam Game Plan*.
- ✦ Avoid blaming; forgive.

- Remember your commitment to your relationship—for better or for worse.
- Think, "We have a dilemma, but we know there's a best solution—let's find it!"

When outside adversity affects a couple's relationship, this may be more challenging to solve. While you're in the process of working through it, and as difficult as it may sound, be kind and empathetic, give each other more hugs and kisses, be generous with verbal affections, and realize that you love this person more than anyone else. No one ever said life would be easy, but when you're a LoveTeam you have someone wonderful to help you through the tough times.

There may be instances when calling in an expert, like a therapist, doctor, or a member of the clergy, can be beneficial. One or both of us may come with baggage that's strong enough so that together we don't have the ability to overcome it. This can include a very dysfunctional upbringing, grief, or past traumatic experiences. Professional help may also be needed if there are addictions, involvement in illegal activities, physical abuse, and other extreme situations.

When we see a beautifully shaped metal work of art, recognize that it started out as a straight piece of iron that was put through fire to mold it into what can now be enjoyed and valued. It's the same with relationships. A LoveTeam usually has to pass through trials to grow and be appreciated. Being a "Snapshots" couple provides a buffer against stress, adversity, and tragedy, and turns potential conflict into a close, unified relationship.

Chapter 27
Forgive and Forget

XOXO

*Forgiveness is not an occasional act,
it is a constant attitude.*
~Martin Luther King, Jr.

On a basketball team, one of the players inadvertently makes their teammate look bad when they throw a bad pass and the intended receiver doesn't catch it. On a winning team, play continues as if nothing happened. Otherwise, the team may lose momentum and a bad trend may begin. Great athletic teams make many mistakes, as do great LoveTeams. Teammates don't get down on them but offer encouragement with, "We'll do better next time!"

Thomas Edison made a lot of mistakes with his inventions but he didn't think of them as failures. He looked at them as progress toward a goal and said, "I have not failed. I've just found more than 1,000 ways that won't work." Patience and perseverance are required whenever we interact with each other because we'll all make mistakes. Even if we only do or say fifty things in a day together, we're bound to make one or more errors. When we give our best effort in spite of occasionally letting our team down, we deserve a clean slate by the end of every day. LoveTeam couples look at overcoming mistakes as part of the process toward the goal of a great relationship.

LoveTeam Amnesia

There's a term most doubles tennis players are familiar with—tennis amnesia. It's a player's ability to temporarily forget a mistake so both partners can keep their concentration on the game. After the pressure is off, they can think about what happened, make appropriate adjustments, and learn from it.

In a relationship, when one partner makes a rather small mistake, the other should have LoveTeam amnesia. Even if they don't say they're sorry, it's up to the other to forgive and forget anyway, especially if it's probably a one-time occurrence. What a wonderful feeling between best friends when we can just let it go.

In volleyball, many teams huddle after each point scored, whether they won the point or not. This gives them all a chance to encourage and support the player who made the error, and for the whole team to get a fresh start. Or, if they made the point, they can celebrate together, which allows them to continue the positive momentum.

In our relationship, we'll have periods when it seems like we've scored a point—positive and growing times. Yes, we'll also have instances of thinking that we've lost a point, when we've had difficulties and not been as close. That's when we need to "huddle," to support and encourage each other, thus growing even stronger than before because of what we've been through together.

Most athletic teams determine a large part of their success by having the highest score at the end of the game. Personal partnerships, on the contrary, determines success partly by having *no score* at the end of every day. Lovemates hold nothing against each other as they start each day, like the zero/zero score at the beginning of a tennis match—Love/Love!

Apologies are Unique

When we make serious mistakes that affect our team, we should feel sorry. These errors may heavily impact our relationship and have long-term implications. For these mistakes, there may need to be more than one apology and a humble attitude as we mend and renew our relationship. We need to "swallow our pride" because our LoveTeam is more important than whether we feel like apologizing or not. Then a positive mood can once again fill our home.

Apologizing is personal and unique, and can take many forms. Certain individuals may feel more comfortable saying, "I'm sorry," or other similar words. Others act sorry but don't actually say any words—it's an implied apology. Still others treat their mate sweeter for a while to make up for the mistake.

No matter what type of apology we use, it's important that we're sincere, we have empathy, and move closer to the other emotionally and physically. Also, we shouldn't make excuses or try to justify doing something wrong when we know it was wrong; this can only make matters worse. In other words, we should take responsibility for what we say and do.

It's always best for the team if the one who made a mistake admits to the other that they were wrong. Also, we should realize that when apologizing, it's really only meaningful if we're determined not to make that mistake again. Otherwise, the words are just wasted breath, and trust will be diminished in the relationship.

An Attribute of Strength

Once there were two men, neighbors in a small community, who years earlier had a disagreement. For the rest of their lives they didn't speak to each other, avoided contact, and didn't wave to each other from their cars, even though that was the custom in their community. One day a son of one of the men asked his father why he was mad at the other man. The father replied, "Hmmm...I can't remember."

How sad that this father set such a bad example of forgiveness for his son. In addition to the negative impact on their children, the two men not only lost the opportunity to have a lasting friendship, they also had to live for years with the stress and negativity this type of attitude produces. Mahatma Gandhi said, "The weak can never forgive. Forgiveness is the attribute of the strong."

Forgiveness is a major part of getting a fresh start in any relationship, but especially in our LoveTeam. If we go to bed with bad feelings, it will be difficult to have a fresh start the next day. Our decision to forgive and forget before going to bed allows for a better night's sleep as well!

Because we're committed for a lifetime, how many times should we forgive and forget? As many times as the other person makes a mistake. However, when it becomes apparent there's a bad trend, it should be identified and lovingly discussed because there may be an underlying reason for what's happening. It then becomes important to work through whatever could be the cause.

Author and businessman, Paul Boese, said, "Forgiveness does not change the past, but it does enlarge the future." See the big picture of mistakes—think of reaching the hundredth step in a stairway as being the point when you become a LoveTeam. Appreciate that we may have gone from step sixty-one to step sixty-eight when we do this process of forgiving correctly. In other words, we will have taken a big leap in becoming a closer couple.

Mistakes are inevitable. Developing LoveTeam amnesia by quickly forgiving and forgetting is part of developing a great relationship. It's better to not emphasize the mistakes that are made. Think of them as part of the learning, growing process of becoming a LoveTeam.

A Closing Note

As this book concludes, our hope for you both is that you have gained the motivation to have a relationship free of conflict and a partnership of closeness. We assure you this can be a reality when you follow *The LoveTeam Game Plan for a loving couple to think, speak, and act like a team* as has been described. As a result, you will know the incredible feeling of being a "Snapshots" couple.

As you proactively apply the team and love concepts, you will be empowered together to decide on cooperative solutions and make your differences become strengths. As best friends and equal partners, you'll find that adversity and tragedies will only draw you closer to each other. At this point, you'll realize that the goal you've desired has been met: you will have achieved a great relationship. What a LoveTeam legacy you will leave for your children and grandchildren!

End Notes

Introduction

1. marriage-councelling.com/marriage-counsellor/2010/marriage-counceling/marriage-councelling-and-the-seven-year-itch-the-real-problem-is-expectations

The Game Plan

2. ohioline.osu.edu/flm01/pdf/FS02.pdf

The Power of Team

3. findarticles.com/p/articles/mi_m3495/is_n2_v42/ai_19224639
4. team-building-bonanza.com/history-of-teamwork.html
5. John Wooden and Jay Carty, *Coach Wooden One-On-One: Inspiring Conversations on Purpose, Passion and the Pursuit of Success* (California: Regal Books, 2003), 162–163.
6. John Wooden and Steve Jamison, *The Essential Wooden: A Lifetime of Lessons on Leaders and Leadership* (New York: McGraw-Hill, 2007), 43.
7. Ezine article, "Building Team Spirit" 01/26/2012 ezinearticles.com/?Building-Team-Spirit&id=900484

"We" Not "Me"

8. John A. Schindler, MD, *How to Live 365 Days a Year: 12 Principles to Make Your Life Richer* (Pennsylvania: Running Press Book Publishers, 2003), 96.
9. Schindler, 94, 95, 138.
10. *Miracle,* prod. Mark Ciardi and Gordon Gray, dir. Gavin O'Connor, 136 min., Disney, 2004, DVD.

Do and Be Our Best

11. Wooden and Carty, *One-On-One,* 163.

An Optimistic Attitude

12. Norman Vincent Peale, *The Power of Positive Thinking* (New York: Random House, 1952), viii
13. Martin E.P. Seligman, PhD, *Authentic Happiness: Using the New Positive Psychology to Realize Your Potential for Lasting Fulfillment* (New York: Simon & Schuster, 2002), 4.
14. nhlbi.nih.gov/whi
15. Pat Blaskower, *The Art of Doubles: Winning Tennis Strategies and Drills* (Ohio: Betterway Books, 2007), 18, 21.
16. Seligman, 5.
17. snopes.com/science/smile.asp

Support Without Regrets

18. Rabbi Pliskin, *Marriage* (New York: Art Scroll, 1998), 30–31.

Basic Principles

19. Richard Carlson, PhD, *Shortcut Through Therapy: Ten Principles of Growth-Oriented, Contented Living* (New York: Penguin Group, 1995), 3.

Commitment and a Climate of Trust

20. http://smallbusiness.chron.com/achieving-commitment-teamwork-exercises-35291.html Frost, Shelley. "Achieving Commitment Teamwork Exercises." SmallBusiness.Chron.com, 6 Nov. 2012.

21. Blaskower, 8.

22. wildfiremag.com/command/teamwork_takes_trust/

Unify Our Needs

23. http://www.feedtherightwolf.org/2012/01/accountability-in-your-marriage

Enjoy Our Differences

24. Paul D. Tieger and Barbara Barron-Tieger, *Just Your Type: Create the Relationship You've Always Wanted Using the Secrets of Personality Type* (New York: Little, Brown and Company, 2000), 4–5.

25. Tieger and Barron-Tieger, 5.

Making Changes and Adjustments

26. www.ghinsberg.com/1m5/the-burmese-monkey-trap.html

27. *Miracle*

28. *Hoosiers*, prod. Carter De Haven, dir. David Anspaugh, 1 hr. 55 min., Hemdale Film Corporation, 1986, videocassette.

Balance

29. Blaskower, 9–10.

Best Friends

30. http://en.wikipedia.org/wiki/Buddy_system

31. *Fever Pitch,* prod. Nick Hornby, et al, dir. Bobby Farrelly and Peter Farrelly, 1 hr. 38 min., 20th Century Fox, 2005, DVD.

Fun and Excitement

32. Seligman, 28.

33. *What About Bob?,* prod. Laura Ziskin and Bernie Williams, dir. Frank Oz, 1 hr. 37 min., Walt Disney Studios, 1991, DVD.

Building a Life Together

34. Blaskower, 3.

Kindness

35. Helen Andelin, *Fascinating Womanhood: How the Ideal Woman Awakens a Man's Deepest Love and Tenderness* (New York: Bantam Dell, 2007), 283.

36. Wooden and Jamison, *The Essential Wooden,* 8.

37. Andelin, 286–287.

Affection

38. everything2.com/user/arianne/writeups/Skin+hunger

39. ziglar.com/newsletter/Zig On…Hugging is the Answer

40. http://marriagegems.com/tag/research-on-touch

Appreciation

41. Hilary Rich and Helaina Laks Kravitz, M.D., *The Complete Idiot's Guide to The Perfect Marriage* (New York: Alpha Books, 2007), 32.

42. Kathleen M. Comerford, "A Hard Look," *Reader's Digest,* November 2011, 35.

43. PsychologyToday.com. 3/02/2004, "The Art of the Compliment: Everyone needs to know how to give and receive compliments."

What Makes Us Tick?
44. Rich and Kravitz, M.D., 11.
45. Stephen R. Covey, *The 7 Habits of Highly Effective Families* (New York: Golden Books, 1997), 211–213.

Communication
46. Blaskower, 130.
47. Ed Young, *Romancing the Home: How to Have a Marriage That Sizzles* (Tennessee: Broadman & Holman Publishers, 1993), 116.
48. Angela Hicks, "Talk Up a Good Marriage," *Prevention Magazine,* December 2008, 107.
49. Nancy Lieberman, *Playbook for Success: A Hall of Famer's Tactics for Business and Leadership* (New Jersey: John Wiley & Sons, 2010), 101.

Cooperative Solutions
50. snicc.org/files/uploads/Facts_about_Swimming_Pool_Drowning_Accidents.pdf

www.ingramcontent.com/pod-product-compliance
Lightning Source LLC
Chambersburg PA
CBHW031245290426
44109CB00012B/438